MW01062634

# Open the Eyes of My Heart

*Embracing the Joys of Everyday Miracles*

Jodie M. Chappuis

Copyright © 2018 Jodie M. Chappuis.

All rights reserved. No part of this book may be used or reproduced by any means, graphic, electronic, or mechanical, including photocopying, recording, taping or by any information storage retrieval system without the written permission of the author except in the case of brief quotations embodied in critical articles and reviews.

This book is a work of non-fiction. Unless otherwise noted, the author and the publisher make no explicit guarantees as to the accuracy of the information contained in this book and in some cases, names of people and places have been altered to protect their privacy.

Scripture texts in this work are taken from the New American Bible, revised edition © 2010, 1991, 1986, 1970 Confraternity of Christian Doctrine, Washington, D.C. and are used by permission of the copyright owner. All Rights Reserved. No part of the New American Bible may be reproduced in any form without permission in writing from the copyright owner.

LifeRich Publishing is a registered trademark of The Reader's Digest Association, Inc.

LifeRich Publishing books may be ordered through booksellers or by contacting:

LifeRich Publishing
1663 Liberty Drive
Bloomington, IN 47403
www.liferichpublishing.com
1 (888) 238-8637

Because of the dynamic nature of the Internet, any web addresses or links contained in this book may have changed since publication and may no longer be valid. The views expressed in this work are solely those of the author and do not necessarily reflect the views of the publisher, and the publisher hereby disclaims any responsibility for them.

Any people depicted in stock imagery provided by Thinkstock are models, and such images are being used for illustrative purposes only. Certain stock imagery © Thinkstock.

ISBN: 978-1-4897-1490-9 (sc)
ISBN: 978-1-4897-1489-3 (hc)
ISBN: 978-1-4897-1491-6 (e)

Library of Congress Control Number: 2018900750

Print information available on the last page.

LifeRich Publishing rev. date: 04/17/2018

*I shall pass this way but once;*
*any good that I can do or any kindness I can show*
*to any human being; let me do it now.*
*Let me not defer nor neglect it, for I shall not pass this way again.*

*- Etienne de Grellet*

# Table of Contents

# *Dedication*

I am dedicating *Open the Eyes of My Heart*, to my mother. There isn't a day that goes by that I don't think about her and miss her. She had so much wisdom and the ability to share it and I know that she is co-writing this with me from the other side. I also have to give my family and friends a big thank you for listening to me and encouraging me all these years. You, George, have always been my rock and I thank God, every day for the Angel in our driveway that brought us together. I have my girls to thank for reasons they won't fully understand until they become a Mom… So I'll thank God for them too. The gift of becoming a Mother is beyond even what I could have imagined. It was truly what inspired me to write this book. I couldn't hold it in, the love in my heart for our girls. Now that our beautiful Anna is married to Joey, who is a blessing to us all, we now have the gift of laughter. He can make Anna laugh and make me laugh even more. He has a heart of gold and truly lives his faith. They work together in youth ministry, and have a love for mission work. They have traveled to the poor far away, but also see the need in our own neighborhoods. Our beautiful and talented daughter, Laura, is also loved and adored. She also has a heart of gold and is very thoughtful and kind. She is engaged to Kyle who fills our lives with adventure. He is unafraid to take on any challenge and has inspired me to finally finish this book. He has helped me tremendously these past few weeks to wrap this up to move it along. Kyle never shy's away from engaging in a stimulating conversation, which I truly enjoy. I've learned so much from these wonderful guys. I love having sons, thank you, Jesus, for continuing to grow our family. By the way, Laura met Kyle in our driveway…the same one where it all began.

One last mention, I must thank the Lord for pushing me to be a confirmation teacher. All those kids, and all those years…I still call them my kids. It was their pushing, yes, the Holy Spirit used them, to plant the seed in my heart and mind. I guess I wasn't the only seed planter. A special thank you to Ava, for reading some of these stories and giving me wonderful encouragement… And to David, my god-son, who helped me get organized, and Ginger who helped me a long time ago…I'm starting to realize this list could get real long. I'm going to say a big thank-you prayer for all the very special people that are gifts to me, my friends and relatives who have had to listen to all of this over the years. Can't forget Conan who taught me how to copy and paste…yea haha. And with my heart still heavy, I have my Sam, who was meant to be in my life, for me to love like a son and will have in my heart forever. I live a life of abundant joy, Lord, and the gift of my faith is the greatest of all.

# Prologue

Sometimes when we try too hard, it is a sign that we need to step back and go a little crazy and wait. I've been trying hard for a long time on this book. Like twenty years to be exact...stop laughing!!

This morning something came to me and it was this. You are having trouble because you aren't comfortable making this about you. What is one of your favorite bible verses? Oh yea, its Matthew 7:7-11...The answer to prayers. Ask and it WILL be given to you; seek and you WILL find; knock and the door WILL be opened to you. For anyone who asks, receives; and the one who seeks, finds; and to the one who knocks, the door will be opened. Which one of you would hand his son a stone when he asks for a loaf of bread, or a snake when he asks for a fish? If you then, who are wicked, know how to give good gifts to your children, how much more will your heavenly Father give good things to those who ask him. Yup, I am officially starting over and changing the title. It's going to be:

*OPEN THE EYES OF MY HEART*

The beauty of our Lord is that He is true love. In all things and in all ways, He loves us. Waiting patiently for things doesn't come easy for us, and yet we expect God to be patient with us! God's wisdom knows no time and only true love will wait until we are ready for Him. Some of us are willing to try to do it on our own for... maybe our whole lives...but God is still there. He never leaves and doesn't barge in... He waits patiently for us to ask. Sometimes we are afraid to ask, maybe because we are afraid of the answer or that there won't be an answer. But in Matthew 7:7-11 it doesn't say maybe or might, it says He WILL. I remember the day I read that and it entered my heart, it changed everything, my heart was opened and I haven't stopped asking! I realized on that day, that nothing is too big or too small for my Lord and my savior. By asking you are saying yes to wanting a relationship with your creator! It opens up dialogue with The One who knows you better than you know yourself. We don't have to be perfect either, in fact being imperfect shows our need for Him.

God does require things from us however. A relationship is no good if it is only one-sided. He requires that we put forth some effort, which is why I must write this stuff down and thankful that He is patient and kind and surpasses all understanding. He told the leper to go dunk seven times, He told the paralyzed man to get up and walk. You get my drift? We don't just magically get everything we want...He knows best, and I'm sure all of us can relate to the fact that many times we were spared from what we thought we wanted and protected from it. We look back and see the reason later in life. But our desire must be real, we must be willing to stand up or get down on our knees to show our desire and love for Him. He even makes that easy...if we don't know how or it feels awkward, we can say, "Help me Lord, I don't know how, please show me."

So, my passion and mission for this earth is to help others come to a relationship with Our Lord Jesus. I have spent the last 30 years working with teens and they have told me over and over to write a book for you see, I have many stories of how the Holy Spirit has worked some cool stuff and it is all in response to prayer. Ask and you shall receive. I am going to try hard to make this not about me. Because truthfully it isn't about me, I came to a complete standstill with this project many times and it's always at the same spot. When I have to put it together and make it my story. Seriously, I was thinking maybe I'm not supposed to do this at all. I have a story I'll tell you later why I know that isn't true. I stop because when it becomes about me then it's as if these things are only possible for me. I would never want others to think there are only certain people God uses. The truth is, God has a plan and purpose for every life He creates, and it's up to us to allow ourselves to be used. It's up to us to open our hearts and our eyes and our ears so that we can feel Him, see Him and hear Him. If you are reading this and you may be the only one…then these words and stories were for you to feel the love of God. Love is, love was and love will always be…GOD IS LOVE.

Thy will be done Lord and thank you Jesus for being you.

I pray for protection for you and me and our families as we grow in Love through Jesus Christ our Lord. Amen

# Introduction

If you're going to pray don't worry if you're
going to worry don't pray the joy in the everyday
miracles

Many little and some not so little miracles, or signs and wonders
some might call them, have been blessings to me. Sometimes the
real miracle is the fact that I didn't miss it. I remember going
for walks, even as a small child, and I would ask the Lord not to
let me miss a thing. Please Jesus, I want to see everything you
have to show me. People would often ask me why these things
happen to me, and why don't these things happen to them. I truly
believe these everyday signs happen for everyone, so the key is to
remember to say your "please don't let me miss anything Lord"
prayer every day. God created us to have a relationship with him,
all we have to do is be open.

So, this first story is funny, like lots of them are, because as
much as we pray and we want to do God's will, we still spend a
lot of our time thinking our will is better. For years I would wake
up, usually around 3 AM, with a nagging thought to write all this
stuff down. Pretty sure this is what they call being called to do
something. Of course, I would ignore it, just lay there, and I'd say
my prayers. I would pray for the people I promised to pray for, but
in the back of my mind was this "please Jodie write this down."

Finally, one afternoon, I was in between customers, and God

was bugging me again in my mind. So, I said to Him, "really God? If you want me to write a book, you'll get me a computer. I can't picture myself writing this book with paper and a pencil." A little bit bratty I know but Jesus knows my heart. Sometimes I treat Him like a dad, and when you look at the Ten Commandments, God is number One, and our parents are number four, so respecting our parents is a big deal. Anyway, because God can be funny, ten minutes after my ridiculous request, my next customer came in the door, sat in my chair and the first thing he said was, "You wouldn't by chance be needing a computer, would you?" I was stunned, all I could think to say was, "Shut up! Are you kidding me? Can I write a book with it?" "Well yeah, it's in my car and I have a printer that goes with it." was his reply. Oh, my gosh, this seems a little too unreal, why am I doubting? God always knows what he's doing. He loves to show himself to us, he delights in us, and desires more than anything to have a relationship with us. Even when we are bratty. So, after giving my friend his haircut, we went out to his car and got the computer. We set it up, remember this is before computers were in every home. That night I started writing my book. The bad news? I don't know how to write a book. I thought I could just write it like I talk. Just keep going. But that wasn't working out. So, after a couple of nights of trying this, I thought well, I'm just going to put it away and will have to just keep praying.

Soon, it started happening again. I was waking up at three or four o'clock in the morning. I had to tell God that it turns out I don't know how to write a book. (Like He didn't already know that.) You are going to have to send me someone, somehow, to help me. I did ask him why He would wake me up so early in the morning/ middle of the night. He said Jodie, this seems to be the only time I can catch you being quiet. Funny!

A couple more days go by, and out of nowhere I hear from Scott, a former student I had in confirmation class. I answered the phone and he's frantically talking, "Jodie, you're not going to believe what happened to me last night. I woke up at two this morning with strict instructions to call you today. I'm supposed to tell you to write a page of miracles today. You cannot hang up until you say yes."

A page of miracles? I was so excited to hear from Scott, but I really had no idea what he was talking about. What does that even mean, a page of miracles, what the heck? He really didn't know either, but he told me he couldn't hang up until I said yes. After a few minutes, I finally just had to agree and say yes, so he could get on with his day. The minute we hung up, of course he called me right back and he said, "it's a table of contents!" Oh...ok, that makes sense... a page of miracles... list my stories, it doesn't have to be one long story. I can do that. "Thank you for calling and thank you for being a listener."

You would think the story was finished here, right? Um, yea, not so much...A few hours went by and my cousin from out West called me with pretty much the same story. She said that she too woke up around two AM. I was a little freaked out and told her to shut up! I guess that's my usual first response. I then told her what Scott had said to me and she couldn't believe it either. Oh, my gosh, OK I will get going Lord, and write our book. Sweet Jesus I will need your help!

John 2:5 *His mother said to the servers, "Do whatever he tells you."*

# When I was three....

God has a purpose for all of us and though I try, I can't help it, I can't keep it in. We all have a mission, and I'm thinking this is mine. Pretty sure when you feel this much love, if you don't share it you explode.

My memory is pretty good, like I remember very detailed things from my childhood. However, I don't remember this event, so I have to take my mother's word for it and so it goes.

It was a warm summer day, and I was just three years old. We were at my grandma and grandpa's cottage. Much of my childhood, especially on Sundays was spent at the lake. My uncles and Godfather were watching me and my cousins along the shore. I was in my inner tube, in the shallow water and I'm sure having a great ol' time, being three and all. I tipped forward and flipped my inner tube and was trapped in the water. I don't know how long it took, but my uncle pulled me out and I was not good. It couldn't have been very long that I was caught underneath my inner tube but my uncles found me and put me on the dock. It was probably just a few seconds but they had to resuscitate me. After I came to, I was in my mom's arms and I said, "Mama Mama I'm up in the clouds with Jesus." What my mother must have felt! Who said parenting was easy? This experience is probably why I've always had an absolute, you cannot talk me out of it love for the Lord and extreme faith. It also might explain my willingness to share it with whoever cares to listen to me. I'll sometimes even share it with people who don't want to listen. That's not so good. Sometimes you have to learn things the hard way. It also might explain why I hated swimming lessons and was terrified of the water until I was ten.

The blessings that came from that day are many. When I close my eyes to pray, I have a picture in my mind, and that picture is of a beautiful green lush Riverbank with a few trees and bright shining light. The way the light shines through the trees and lights up the meadow just brings me to a really peaceful place. The best part, is that I'm in the lap of my Lord Jesus. His arm is around me and I'm in the happiest place I could be....in His lap!! This has always been the picture, ever since I was a little girl when I close my eyes to pray. Sometimes I wonder if that was actually heaven, or just a place that the Lord took me for a really short time. I guess it doesn't matter because the feeling I had and still have when I close my eyes is a warm and tender love. My memory kicked into gear from that point on. I can remember some minute details of every period of my life. One that comes to me right now is lying under our birch tree in our yard feeling the wonderful warm sun and watching the breeze moving the small leaves. They sound so peaceful. The simple things are my most favored. I remember thinking that I love my life, my eyes and my ears, the smell of summer and the feel of the grass.

My Love for Jesus entered my heart on that day when I was three.

Psalm 116:17 *I will offer a sacrifice of praise and call on the name of the Lord*

# Beauty School drop out?

## (Not me)

So, do you guys remember the movie Grease? And the song Beauty School Dropout? Yeah that's kind of what kept me in school for the first while. Ever since the second grade I knew I wanted to do hair for a living. Mainly because I wanted to have something in my home so I could be with my kids. However, I wasn't prepared for how much I was going to hate beauty school. The funny thing is, I really couldn't blame school so much, it was my attitude. You see I had a strange thing happened to me when I was 15 years old. I went through menopause. Puberty and menopause at the same time, it's no wonder God built up and had me trusting HIM at my young age. Because through all of this, Jesus was my rock. My Faith is what got me through the battle of my negative attitude and crazy hormones.

And the story goes… I hated my life, I hated school, pretty much hated myself. Even though I had faith and I knew I was loved, I still had a negative attitude. It was almost like I was in a dark tunnel. Like there just weren't enough windows. Couldn't sleep, I tossed and turned with terrible insomnia, and eventually was taking Valium to sleep at night. I was given the valium and told to take a quarter of a pill to sleep. I did this only two times because I felt so drowsy and even more foggy and in the dark than I did before. Nothing seem to be helping me. So, I called home,

3

which back then we didn't do that much. I think of it now and it cracks me up. It would cost like a quarter or something for every minute. That's probably not right, but it was something like that. My mom answered, and in all her wisdom, knew just what to say. She started yelling at me. She hollered, "Jodie!!" Because of course I was bawling and she had to be abrupt. "Are you praying?" "Of course, I'm praying mother, but I don't think God really gives a rip." Then she said, "Are you worried?" "Yes, I'm really worried!" You see she didn't know I had a whole handful of Valium and was ready to just take them all right then and there. She could hear me crying, bawling, and she knew I was desperate. She hollered, "Jodie, if you're going to pray don't worry and if you're going to worry don't pray. Go to bed go to sleep and when you wake up the answer will be there!" and she hung up on me. So, I did what she said. (I took the pills and threw them in the garbage) then I went into my room and I laid flat on the floor. I told the Lord that he could do whatever he wanted with me. I belong to him. I want what you want Lord!! I finally stopped crying and I went to bed and slept the best I had slept in years. Remember my hormones had been screwed up since the 8th grade. I woke up around 5 o'clock and the answer came to me, call Laure. I thought the polite thing was to wait until at least 6 AM, But couldn't wait so at 5:45, I called Laure, who by the way I barely knew. She was someone that was in my class that I hadn't made friends with yet. So basically, I was calling an acquaintance to ask if I could come and live with her at 6 o'clock in the morning. Turns out it was perfect timing, because she lives with her fiancé's aunt, and Dottie was just about to leave the house to go nanny for her daughter. She left every day at six and got home every night at eight. Laure was ecstatic, she was so happy to have somebody come and live with her because she was all alone in the house most of the time. God really knew what he was doing, (duh) he put me in a house with a person who had so much faith and lived her faith to the extreme every single day. She never believed that God wanted anything bad for us. Even a cold. She would not let it get her, and would go through all the stages of a cold in one day. She had so much trust and faith in the Lord!! Everything my mother had taught me, everything I thought I already knew but I obviously was in a major growth spurt (kick in the pants) in my faith. You would think the story would end here… But no… The Lord had even more for me.

I still was not too sure if I like the beauty business. My attitude was much better but still needed confidence in what I was doing. After Christmas and for a few months, the students of the school were practicing on their models for a competition that was coming up. I wasn't too excited about it, I'm not a very competitive person, and I wasn't even sure if I liked doing hair. But it was something we had to do. So, the night before the competition, I drove down to Faribault, about a two-hour drive, where my friend Janet lived and still went to school. She had beautiful silky blonde hair and was a beautiful person. She thought it would be great to miss some school and agreed to come up and be a model for me. The night before the competition I practiced on her just one time. Of course, having lived with Laure for a few months, I knew that I needed to pray first. I had no idea what I was going to do with her hair but after having said a prayer, an idea popped into my head! I could make her hair swoop up to the side gather together with the big seashell and make it look like a waterfall!! OK let's go with that. Janet who knew her hair better than anyone gave me a few pointers, and in no time this unique and very cool hairstyle appeared. Her hair was very long and being so blonde, the degree of difficulty was pretty high. To make a long story short, the competition was fierce, about 60 of us, and of course everyone wanted to win. I was just happy to get through it. I ended up, yeah you know it, winning first place! It was so awesome I was given a big trophy, (was wishing for cash but the trophy was nice!) All I could think was… God is a riot! He really loves me! Except wait a minute, now I have to go to a national convention and compete against licensed stylists, the second-place winner and me!!!

It happened to be in Minneapolis the next weekend and I should've been nervous. Why wasn't I nervous? Oh yeah...I prayed and not gonna worry. It was in a great big convention hall and I had to stand on a platform along with 30 or 40 other professional stylists from all over the United States. Most of them with professional models as well. Being the only student in the competition I tried to look like I belonged, but I'm wearing my pink chino pants with my Hawaiian top (to go with my waterfall theme), and all the other stylists were decked out with a lot of diamonds and very dressed up it was pretty funny. There were people in a balcony above us watching and the room was full of hundreds of people. I still wasn't nervous, I said my prayer I trusted in God, and I just wanted to get through it. I was thinking that nobody was really paying attention to me anyway. It wasn't until I took the pipe cleaners out of Janet's hair and heard everyone's reaction that I realize they were actually watching me...this was funny to me. I guess I did pray for God to do something to help me feel more confident in what I was doing. I'm picturing myself right now back on that stage and Janet, breaking out in hives because she was getting nervous and all I could think was God's got a plan God's got a reason just help me get through it.

The judges were from all around the world, and after we finished, and time was up, the judges took over. People were coming up to me, handing me their business cards and telling me I had a really good chance. I wasn't shy about letting the Lord take all the credit. I would respond to all these people with well if God wants it then it will be.

Later in the afternoon, we all gathered to hear the results of the competition in a great big ballroom. It had huge beautiful chandeliers and seating for at least a thousand. I was sitting in a chair with my dad and mom, my sister, and a bunch of classmates just waiting for it all to be over. I have to be honest and confess that I was a little bit excited to think that maybe I might've placed in the top three. Did I mention that everyone was a professional?

OPEN THE EYES OF MY HEART

They called third-place, nope not me. They called second-place, not me. They called first place, what!?! They called my name! It was unreal!!! I couldn't believe it I sat there stunned by dad tried getting me up off the chair and as I started walking toward the stage I realize that both of my legs were sound asleep. Could this not have happened at a worse time? Both of my legs were like 10 pounds heavier and way out in front of me...I was laughing because I knew God was trying to lighten me up and keep me humble. I made it to the stage and don't think I've ever heard my dad yell so loud. We were all pretty excited. Most of all, it was a really great moment because I was overwhelmed with extreme love knowing that I was doing the right thing with my life. I've use that story so many times over the 30 years I've done hair. It's not a story about how great I am at what I do, it's a story about recognizing that even when you're at your lowest, God has a reason for every day that you're alive. It doesn't have to be big, cuz even very small things when done with great love can change the world. It also taught me that the things we are given and the miracles that happen to us are meant for us to share with each other. It is how He grows His kingdom. Thank you, Jesus, for the love and wisdom of my mother for the gift of Laure my friend but mostly for the gift of faith because it truly can move mountains! One thing I forgot to mention, the night that my mom hung up on me, she spent the entire night on her knees praying for me!! THERE IS POWER IN PRAYER...it saves lives amen!!

> Acts 2:28 *You have made known to me the paths of life; you WILL fill me with joy in your presence*

# Here's a funny cow story

*(This story cracks me up. God enjoys a good laugh too.)*

I was 19 when I finished beauty school, and I felt a little bit too young to get serious about my career. My girlfriend Nancy, who to this day is still one of my very best friends, was going to school in Denmark. This meant I wouldn't see her for almost a year and that seemed like a long time. Her parents were going to be visiting her in February, and we all thought it was a good idea for me to tagalong. I didn't want to get a serious job in the hair biz, wasn't ready for that yet, a job in retail seemed perfect. However, I wasn't making enough money even though working full-time. I took it to prayer... I remember saying God, what should I do.?? Do you want me to get another job? I'll do whatever you want me to do. Please don't let me miss any of the things, the signs that will guide me to the right answer. After having said this prayer I do remember just working all the time, not really thinking too much about getting another job...I was too busy. Then one day, I looked out our window and there stood a big cow in our front yard. This made me laugh, but I also knew what I had to do. I hollered for my dad, and together we went outside to try and get this cow corralled. This might sound easy, it's not. The two of us were laughing, while ridiculously trying to convince this big huge animal that she needs to be someplace safe. This wasn't one of our cows, so a little part of me was somewhat annoyed that we had to put it within our fence. Good thing it was a beautiful day!! Dad said it was to keep it safe until we find out who it belongs to. He called all the neighbors, he called the radio station, he called the sheriff and nobody claimed her. I didn't know about any of this, but four days before my trip, a check came in the mail that my dad gave to me. It was a little bit sad to think that God sent a cow to be butchered for me. But it isn't the first time that God sacrificed something of HIS to make our lives better. I had more than enough money for my trip, with some leftover. Kind of goes along with that Bible verse, you know the one where God gives you what you need pushed down and overflowing. We are so quick to minimize God's abilities, and His willingness to supply all our needs. He wants so much more for us than we want for ourselves. Praying for His will is actually hard for us to do because we think He doesn't know our wants and our desires. But not only does he know our wants and our desires He knows what's best and can bring it. Thank you, Jesus, for my holy cow!! Amen

Psalm 37:4 *Find your delight in the Lord who WILL give you your heart's desire*

# George

I could go on and on about George. The stories I have shared so far have really been God not just showing Himself to me, but growing my faith. He knows he doesn't have to prove Himself to me. He knows how much I love him. But what's great about God is he loves to show us how much He loves us.

I remember meeting George when I was 12 years old and he was 18. Thankfully he doesn't remember meeting me because that would just be weird. After high school some of my girlfriends had a crush on him and I thought to myself, yea he's cute but isn't he a little too old?

Then on a warm summer evening, my girlfriends and I were sitting on the porch at Suebee's house questioning if we would ever get married and who that person would be. We were all back from college for the summer and we had stuff to talk over. My friend Suebee had a letter she had gotten from someone at school. She passed it around…it was a letter from God, it was called God's plan for your mate. You know… I think I'll share it with you, I still have a copy of it and I still pass it out to lots of people. I'm not sure who wrote it, but years later, I found it in the theology of the body book that we used for confirmation class which was written by Saint Pope John Paul II. So maybe it's something he wrote. I guess I should put written by anonymous, but pretty sure it was written by the Holy Spirit.

Here it goes ….

Everyone longs to give themselves completely to someone, to have a deep soul relationship with another, to be loved thoroughly and exclusively. But God to a Christian says, no, not until you're satisfied and fulfilled and content with living loved by me alone. I love you my child and until you discover that only in me is your satisfaction to be found, you will not be capable of the perfect human relationship I have planned for you. For you will never be united with another until you are united with me. Exclusive of any longings, I want you to stop planning, stop wishing and allow me to give you the most thrilling plan existing… The one that you can't imagine, I want you to have the best. Please allow me to give it to you. Just keep watching me, expecting the greatest things… Keep experiencing that satisfaction knowing that I am. You must wait… Don't be anxious, don't worry. Don't look around at the things others have gotten or that I've given them. Don't look at the things you want. Just keep looking off and away up to me, or you will miss what I want to show you. And then, when you are ready, I'll surprise you with a love far more wonderful than any you have ever dreamed of. For you see, until you are ready and until the one I have for you is ready, I am looking even at this very instant to have you both ready at the same time. Until you are both satisfied exclusively to experience the love that exemplifies your relationship with me, and this is perfect love. And my beloved, I want you to have this most wonderful love, I want you to see in the flesh a picture of your relationship with me, and to enjoy utterly and concretely the everlasting union a beauty and perfection and I love that I offer you with myself, know that I love you utterly!

So yeah, that was the letter that we read and we all decided that we would just let it go and let the Lord find us whoever He wanted us to be with. Good plan, live your life being happy to be yourself!!

It was about a week later, God and His humor had my car break down. Something led me to George's gas station to have my tire fixed. George's gas station wasn't a fix-it station so it was a little funny when I pulled up with this flat tire issue. The good news was, my mom's office was right behind his station. I was moving up to Minneapolis to live with my friend Nancy, with twenty dollars to my name and no job yet. Trusting always in all things.

George said he couldn't replace my tire but he could change it for me. I thought that was a very nice thing being I had a really nice spare tire in my trunk... back in those days you needed a separate key for your trunk, which I didn't have. Mike and Gary thought it was funny to throw my trunk key in the trunk. My car was packed to the max and there was no way to get to my spare tire. So, I went over to my mom's office to borrow 20 more dollars... Yay! now I have $40! When I got back to George's station my car had been returned with a brand-new tire. I told him I couldn't afford a new tire and he said that they, the tire store right behind his station, replaced it because the tire was defective. Good story huh? I bought it. God's Holy angels were so busy setting all this in motion. I hopped in my car and thought that was just great news and sped away thinking... God blesses, that's what God does!! I have forty bucks for some groceries and a new tire! I moved to Minneapolis that day, but came home every weekend to get gas for my car!

The story goes on, months later, my friend Margie had the girls over for dinner and George was across the street with the boys having a chili party. Needless to say, the party ended up in Margie's driveway. (Unreal to think that someday we would live in this very house. Yup, after twenty years of marriage we bought the house with the special matchmaker angel in the driveway.)

We started dating a short time later and the rest is history. It turns out George was a believer and just the right person for me. We had no idea at the time just how much our faith was going to play such an important role and lead us to our family. God had and will always have the best plan.

And the story goes on… Before we became engaged is when I found out that I had gone through early menopause, I was not able to have children. The babies that had been in my heart since I was five. I fully expected George to move on and leave me, but the day we found out changed my life forever. George was in the middle of a softball game he was standing at shortstop and I came to sit in the bleachers. He knew what had gone on that day, that I was going to get the results of my tests and he did a thumbs up from the infield, wondering if it was good news and I had to do a thumbs down. Trying very hard to hold back the tears. He ran off the field in the middle of the game and grabbed me and we drove away. We found a place to sit on the edge of a cliff high above the lake and cried. I had no idea if he would stay with me or not. In fact, I encouraged him not to knowing how badly he wanted to be a dad and what a good dad he would make. He told me he wanted little girls with long legs and I told him I always wanted little boys with baseball caps. We sat there till it got dark, this beautiful summer evening will always be in my memory. As we watched the beautiful sunset, we held each other saying over and over… God must have a plan. All along God was building our faith, he knew this was coming, so it was in Him that we had to put our trust.... And here is where our Story really begins!!!

Perseverance in Trial

James 1:2 *Consider it all joy, my brothers, when you encounter various trials*

# *Anna*

I was always told that God has a plan and everything happens for a reason. How many times have you heard me say that so far? Like we really shouldn't question why or how come. He has a plan. He has different ways of showing Himself to us but then again, He shows Himself to us in similar ways. He uses nature, He uses people, He stirs up our hearts. Mom used to say that we shouldn't deny ourselves listening to the stranger in the elevator, it might just be God talking to you about something you need to hear. These days we teach our children to be afraid of strangers and not to speak to them. Also, true sometimes... But if we learn to listen to our little voice and trust our instincts we can experience joy in some amazing ways. Otherwise, we become a society of detachment, disengaged in other people. God needs us to be his hands and feet and words sometimes. Others can be that for us too. This kind of takes me into my next story.

Right after George and I got married, we started the process of adoption. Not a day went by, that I didn't try something ... try to get on a list or make a contact to somehow get the ball rolling. At the time, Minnesota was one of two states that it was nearly impossible to adopt a baby. We tried everything. I prayed and prayed and prayed some more. There were so many nights I would lie in bed and silently cry myself to sleep. I knew God would not have placed this desire on our hearts if he had no plans to follow through for us.

Through all of my research I learned there were 13 million couples on a list for adoption in our country. We went to a lobbyist group in Minneapolis trying to change the laws in our state. Every agency was not taking names, international adoption, domestic and even the religious affiliations were not accepting names. We were told by one organization that we had to be married four years before they would take our names. After that four years, it was going to be at least an eight year wait. So, you're saying twelve years? This seemed so unreal. There were hundreds of people at the meeting in Minneapolis hoping for some answers. It brought to light the true facts which are, there is no such thing as an unwanted pregnancy. There were so many people there who were as desperate and sad in their hearts as we were.

It's hard to explain, we live in a world that doesn't really talk about what it's like for the couple who suffers with infertility. We live in a world where people say things like well you're lucky you don't have to worry about birth control. Or people would say "you want mine?" My response was always "only if you mean it! I'll take them!" After two years of trying to get on a list, I started to feel like maybe this wasn't something God wants for us. I started to feel sorry for myself, thinking geez Lord I didn't smoke, I didn't drink, I didn't have sex, I didn't do drugs! All because I wanted to stay healthy and have a safe place to grow a baby inside of me... George is going to be a great dad!! You need to help us Lord.

I started to feel resentment toward my friends who had gotten married years after we had and they were having babies. I was feeling very helpless!! I decided to start a novena to Saint Jude helper of the helpless. It's a good one you want me to share it with you? Okay it goes like this:

May the sacred heart of Jesus be adored glorified loved and preserved throughout the whole world now and forever. Sacred Heart of Jesus pray for Us, Saint Jude worker of miracles pray for us, Saint Jude helper of the helpless pray for us, thank you Saint Jude.

I prayed that prayer nine times a day for weeks and weeks. Months and months...And then it happened, a friend of a friend named Judy came to our aid. She was a nurse at the clinic, who had talked to a lady named Jean just the day before. Jean was a retired social worker who had done adoptions in the seven-state area!!! She was a total stranger (not in an elevator but close) and somehow the conversation happened between she and Judy. Somehow God had to arrange for us to bump into Judy and somehow, I had to spill my guts about wanting a baby. (That's not that hard to imagine) and that's when Judy shared her story about Jean... the very day after she met Jean!!

We got Jean's number from Judy and George immediately made the call to Jean. In a week, she was at our house writing up our study and promising that it would work out, that we would get our baby. It all happened so fast. First, we waited and waited then whoosh! So excited to just be on a list! Thank you, St Jude, for your prayers. We made it to a list!! And it was a woman named Judy... did anyone else catch that? Stay with me people.

Now at least we waited feeling hopeful. God has a plan. Everything happens for a reason. All those one liners that my mother would speak, we were completely trusting. Believing without doubt. All the waiting taught us so many things. How much do you need us to know lord?

Waiting upon the Lord is a blessing. Its precious time spent with Him, it's like a tree during a drought, the roots have to grow deep to reach its nourishment.

Two years later, another friendship was growing and that was my love for Saint Theresa. She was my confirmation saint and I felt her tugging on my heart so I began praying with her. I also have a love for Saint Therese', She's known as the little flower. She passed away at a very young age and she made it her mission to unite heaven and earth by sending a flower to those in need. Obviously, I had a need. I remember the first time that I prayed to her, I asked specifically for a rose. Later, in that same day I had a customer come and was a few minutes late. She explained that she was halfway to my house but had to turn around because she felt like bringing me a rose! I had no idea that she grew roses in her backyard but on that day that Rose meant everything to me. Another time, I had prayed to saint Therese and of course asked for a rose. I was out for my daily walk with my golden retriever... We were on a gravel road and she decided to go potty. My walks were great because it was my morning prayer time. I was waiting for princess to do her thing and praying with Saint Therese', kind of giving her the business for not sending me a rose that week. I have a bucket of dried roses in my house from St. Therese' but sometimes I would just see a rose and that was good enough for me. Felt like teasing her a bit on this particular morning. So while waiting for the dog on the gravel road I looked down and there in the gravel was a plastic rose!! In perfect shape but covered in gravel. So funny!!! The thought that came to me was it has been here all week Jodie. Looks like she wanted to give me the business too!! Oopsie. Thank you so much. Love you girl!!

It was early June 1988 and once again, just like every day I had handed everything over to my Lord. Saint Teresa was letting me know she was there with me praying for me. I know this, but you go through different feelings while waiting for the Lord…. We all go through different things in our lives that for some reason it seems like God's not hearing our prayers. But in His timing things come around. Months went by and now it's February 1989 it was my Mom's birthday and I remember taking in EPT test because I could have sworn I was pregnant. It happened every now and then where I would think I was pregnant but on this day, I actually went to the store and bought a pregnancy test. About a week later a good friend and customer of mine passed away in a car accident. She was only 20 years old, her name was Pam, and she was one of the most special people I've ever known. She was in a terrible accident after coming home for her dad's 50th birthday. Her parents were about two minutes behind the accident and one of the first ones on the scene. It was so tragic. Losing my dear friend made my negative EPT test seem not so bad. She was the kindest person. Always thoughtful, very kind. I mean she would bring shamrock cookies on St. Patrick's Day, pumpkin cookies on Halloween and here she had this horrible accident and gave away her heart at Valentine's. If we could see Heaven we would never question why these very special people get to go.

One month later, I remember we were on our way to the baptism of our little Goddaughter named Madeline, it was pouring rain outside and I was feeling especially sorry for myself. We were going to name our little girl Madeline. Before leaving I remember my mom saying, "Jodie, knock it off! You must realize that when you can genuinely be happy for other people then the lord will be able to give you what you want. It will show him that you're ready" Easy for her to say she got to have three babies. I didn't exactly receive the message right away, my roots needed to get a little deeper. So, on the drive over, in the pouring rain it came to me. It was an hour drive and I bawled most of the way. George kept asking me if I was going to pull it together or if we should turn around. I kept thinking we can't turn around! We are the God parents! I don't know if it was all the rain coming down or what, but I felt like my roots hit bottom and found water. Lord I'm so sorry! Please forgive me, I am genuinely over-the-top happy to have this baby Goddaughter name Madeline.

When we got there, I stepped out of the car and the sun came bursting through the big dark clouds. I knew God heard me and He was OK with it. George just stood there, kind of looking at me like oh my gosh look at that sun, it's beaming and after all my crying, my make-up was fine. You know how you look after bawling? Yea, I looked normal (and I use the word normal loosely ha)

After all these little, though powerful, everyday miracles that God used to keep us going, keep us praying and got me sharing its now our fifth anniversary, May 26, 1989!!

I was busy cutting hair in my in-home salon, when the

florist came with a dozen roses from George. As they were being delivered the phone rang...it was the lady from the adoption agency wondering if she could come and see us later in the afternoon. Umm sure. I was a little curious as to what she would want. We had just talked to her two weeks before, to update our study. It had been two years since Jean wrote it up and she had since retired for real. We were her very last study by the way and did I mention that she had the best placement record as a freelance adoption worker in the state? Ya. God only sends the best!! Anyway, I said sure I'm getting done work early today so 3:30. It seemed like a good time for her to come. Did you catch that the roses were delivered at the same time the phone call came? Yea, So On with the story... I was being a little bit bratty... for our Anniversary, George wanted to go to the Twins game that night and come home. I thought it would be better if we went to the Twins game and stayed up in the cities and bum around. Around 3 o'clock, when I got through with work, I called my mom. I felt the need to nag. She always had a way of putting me in my place and snapping me out of it!! She said "Jodie! You are ruining your special occasion by trying to make it special. Hang up the phone and let the Lord make your day special." So, I hung up the phone I got on my knees and I said Lord make my day. (With a bit of sarcasm) ...Soon, George came home and after a few minutes Ellen came to our door. She saw the flowers on the table and asked what the flowers were about. When I told her, it was our fifth anniversary she got a little choked up...this made me feel bad because I thought maybe her husband just died or something. She quickly pulled out a picture of this beautiful little tiny baby and handed it to us. I looked at her asked "whose baby is this?" You see Jean used to bring pictures of babies and leave them on the table just to keep us hoping and praying and realizing that it's going to happen. Ellen said, "well she's yours if you can go pick her up on Tuesday"!! What? Oh, my gosh!!! George and I looked at each other we both started crying we couldn't believe it! Can this really be happening? I got up to go to

19

the kitchen to get Kleenex and I bashed into the door. I practically knocked myself out. We both were laughing and crying all the same time especially when we realized that she was born on the day of my mother's birthday. February 4th, the day that I took my EPT test, the day that I felt like I was pregnant, that was the day she was born!! Only God could've arrange such a beautiful thing. There has not been a day that goes by that I don't thank the Lord for His wonderful ways! For making us wait, it was time for us to grow as a couple it was time for us to grow in our faith. I used to say way back in high school that couples should wait five years after marriage to have kids…It was our fifth anniversary!!!! God was cluing me in on the plan. I just had no idea. Why would I have said that? That was a stupid thing to say!

We had less than 1% chance to adopt a child and there hadn't been an adoption in our county in eight years. God has a plan for every single baby he makes. I really feel like that's what's wrong with birth control, It makes people think that they are the ones who are the creators. I swear all of these thoughts were cruising through my head all in a split second!! I had literally asked everyone I knew to pray for us and for the beautiful person that was going to have to make the hard decision in order for our child to get to us. For every abortion, there are hundreds of parents waiting for the souls of their children to get to them.

So, needless to say, we had the biggest party our house had ever seen. We didn't go to the Twin's game and God really did make our day special. All the many people that I asked to pray for us sent gifts. We were so thrilled beyond words but nobody was more thrilled than my mom! Anna was born on her birthday, the day she never wanted to celebrate. It was a sad day for her entire life because it was when her own mother died. This gift of a first grandchild was a gift from heaven for us all. All children are gifts from heaven. Thank you, Jesus! We got the house ready for our beautiful baby Anna!!

Forgot to mention that Anna was called "little rosebud" and

it's ok to tell your story to a complete stranger. You never know who God will choose to deliver your roses.

> Numbers 6:24-26 *The Lord bless you and keep you! The Lord let His face shine on you and be gracious to you! The Lord look upon you kindly and give you peace!*

# My Mom

I really don't feel like I can go any further without talking about my Mother. She was the best mom anyone could ever ask for. Growing up with Patsy as my mom was one of my great blessings. She was the kind of mom that always wanted to get to know my friends, she was the kind of person that always saw the good in others, and would take the time to have the long conversations. My sisters and I always knew how blessed we were.

Her story could be a book all by itself. You see she had it rough from the very beginning. Her mother died shortly after she had given birth to my mom. My mom had twin brothers that were three years old when she was born and back in those days, it was unusual for the dad to take care of the children by himself. They were either put in orphanages or family took care of them. In my mom's case, she and her brothers were taken in by her grandmother. Her mom's mom, who had already raised 11 children. Well, not really, one died at birth and two young boys drowned in the lake at the ages of nine and ten. She also lost her husband six years later in the same lake. Imagine taking in twin three year olds and a newborn infant right after losing your daughter. Martha, my mom's mom, was only 29 when she passed. By the way my Grandma Martha was a writer, and I'm sure she has something to do with the nagging I feel to do this book.

I used to love when my mom would tell stories of what it was like for her on the farm. She would talk of walking home from school through the fields singing songs, listening to the birds, enjoying the sky, and then to walk into the home where her grandma was and the smell of supper would fill her heart with joy. The boys would have chores outside and my mom would help her grandma with the indoor chores. She learned how to cook from her grandmother who was really like her mom. I used to think about how weird it must've been to never even say the word mom. She always spoke so lovingly of her grandmother, and those years with such tenderness, she never felt sorry for herself. Because the family is so large, I remember lots of funerals and weddings as a kid. The older aunts and uncles would usually bring up my Grandma's funeral. They would talk about it as being the saddest funeral of all. They placed my mom in a bassinet on top of the casket for the wake. What a picture that would put in my mind. It was no wonder my sisters and I were so thankful and appreciative of our Mom.

When Mom turned seven, her grandmother got sick with cancer. My mom continued to live there, with her brothers that were now ten. When she got home from school the wonderful scent of dinner was not there. She was the one to make the dinner now. Mom slept in the same bed with her grandma, gave her grandma her medicine, and would get up during the night to take her grandmother to the bathroom. This went on until my mom was 10 years old. To this day I don't know what it was like for my uncles, they lived in the house too, I know that they continued to do all the chores outside. I can imagine it was very hard for them because they now were 13 and probably expected to be adults. I just know for my mom it was just her life. This woman that she loves so dearly, that she slept with in the same bed, would as my mom would say "wipe her fanny" right up until the night before she died. Cancer took her down to 68 pounds until it finally took her completely away from my mom. While she was on her walk home somehow, she heard that her Grandma had died. She talked about how she ran and ran. She felt like her legs would fall off when she finally got to the house. She walked into the front room to find all her aunts and uncles there. She was told to go to the back room. There she sat all by herself, while the others grieved their mother, she was in the back room grieving the same woman, alone. Mom rarely talked about this night in her life. She did say one time "where were these people when grandma was sick?" Thinking about that now, as an adult, I imagine they took care of their mother during the day while mom was at school, but to a ten-year-old who was sleeping in the same bed with someone that sick, Well I guess that's just the way they did things back then. She had a tea set and a doll and sat in the back room to grieve all by herself.

The arrangements that were made and I'm sure they meant no harm, but her brothers were put in a family and were able to stay together. The cousins that my uncles stayed with took them in as sons. They lived in a town about 30 miles away and Mom would get to visit them in the summertime. My mother was taken to Faribault where she lived with an aunt who had two daughters and they really didn't want another one. Mom was made to get herself up and walk to school early every day so she could make it in time for mass. It was at least a 2-mile walk, which isn't made up story. You know the one that our parents would walk ten miles and is was uphill both ways? Anyway, they would pass her on their way to work and wouldn't pick her up to give her a ride. It could be pouring rain, below zero, it really didn't matter, she walked all by herself every day and made it in time for church. Of course, Mom had fond memories of walking down the street. Singing and smelling the fall trees or the fresh air after a rain. She felt comfort in the Lord and noticed Him in the simple things. After schoo,l she would walk to the bakery where she had a job frosting donuts, then walk home. Hard to imagine that this is just a little 10-year-old girl, (which by the way, she didn't get to bring her doll or tea set with her from the farm.) When she got home from the bakery, they would have already finished eating dinner and the dishes were waiting. She would go into her bedroom to do her homework only to find the laundry there waiting for her to fold and put away. I always wondered if they wrote the story of Cinderella about Mom's life. The funny thing about her is she never complained. I know she was hurting and sad, she would tell us the stories not in a way that would make us feel sorry for her because she always had such joy. This was her life. I would ask her "mom, how come you aren't mad at God? You should have been mad at him." She always answered with the same answer, "No Jodie, everything I went through made me love Jesus even more. I knew He is always with me and My mother did more for me from heaven than she ever could have on earth. I prayed to her every night as I cried myself to sleep, knowing I wasn't alone, feeling her spiritually with me everywhere I went." This is how I was brought up... with a mother with such deep love and spiritual knowledge, she never doubted, and making it to mass every day, ended up being the best thing that her aunt and uncle could have done for her. Receiving the Eucharist every day was what was giving her the strength, knowledge, wisdom, understanding, right judgment, and true love for the Lord. She grew up in a time when The Catholic Church wasn't as spiritual at least not outwardly. But my mom always had a real spiritual awareness and deep devotion. She would talk about these times with sadness but also strangely didn't feel sorry for herself. The Catholic church is big on the fruits of suffering. When I watch the Passion of the Christ, I'm always so drawn to Simon of Cyrene, he was dragged out of the crowd to help Jesus with the cross. Of course, he didn't want the cross at first, he was forced to take it. After he made the trek with our lord, he didn't want to let it go. His relationship with Jesus was so intimate that he was sad for it to end. Nobody wants to suffer, but it changes us for the better if we allow ourselves to carry it with Christ.

Mom often talked about how much she wished she would have been adopted. What that would've been like to live in a family that truly wanted her. After she met my dad, he whisked her away. She was ready to start the second half of her life. To have the family she always longed for and to be for my sisters and I the best Mom ever.

> John 1 :4-5 *Through him was life, and this life was the light of the human race; the light shines in the darkness, and the darkness has not overcome it*

# *Unless we become like a child*

Every single day, since the day Anna came to our home, my mom would come over for a visit. She worked in the insurance office where George worked, and we had the best time watching Mr. Rogers at lunch, going for walks after work, even getting groceries together. She would get worried that she was spending too much time with us, that she might be overstaying her welcome. But her love of her little granddaughter especially when we thought it was never going to happen was such a joy. George was great about it too, he always loved when she was in the house, he would joke about being the luckiest guy in the office because he got to go to work and kiss the secretary every day.

My mom had been a smoker, and it always bothered her, she really wanted to quit. She was given the patch and back then the patch was brand-new, hers had a high amount of nicotine and she was in pain from it almost from the very beginning. She knew something wasn't right, she also knew that she reacted from all medications. She was very allergic to penicillin. She didn't last with the patch very long and was still having pain. Mom went to the Dr. for an annual physical. Her physical health was always a worry for her. I think the trauma of watching her grandmother die not to mention not having a mother to go to was not easy for sure. Also, forgot to mention that her dad, who only visited on Christmas Eve every year, passed away when she was eight years old…on Christmas Eve. So she only got to see him seven times in her life. They said he died of a broken heart.

Anyway, as usual they found her to be in great health with the heart of an 18 year- old. Good news you would think but the doc gave her an antidepressant for the pain. She knew the pain wasn't in her head and she refused to take the drugs. Mom decided to go to an internist, and it was there that they discovered she had pancreatic cancer. She was at the doctor by herself and so shocked by this news. Her intuition was telling her something was wrong, but stage four cancer? Not in a million.

On this same day, George and I were dealing with our little three-year-old Anna, she had some kind of virus with a high fever. Anna had never been sick. So we were a little panicky to say the least. Little did we know that Anna was being used by God to show us our first sign. You see, her fever had reached 104 and we were told to put her in the bathtub. When we took her out of the tub it didn't go down very much maybe to 102. At the same time, we got the phone call, thankfully George took it for me, mom was calling us to come over. I knew something was wrong George hung up the phone looked at me and was white as snow. He had already lost his mother to cancer and he said "I don't want to lose another mother." This also was the anniversary of his own mother's death.

This story is kind of long and very hard for me even though it's been 23 years. I tell it often, to my confirmation classes, they were the ones who kept encouraging me to write a book. So, this is for all my kids and ninth graders past and future.

My mom's faith journey and the things that happened to her along the way have changed the lives of many people in these 23 years. This book is really all about the everyday little wonders and signs that God gives us to deal with whatever is in front of us. Some of them I would classify as a miracle mostly because they can create a conversion in your heart and soul. How a person receives it or whatever message they get from it is really the miracle. All the things leading up to this time is just God's love and preparation. He knew how badly I wanted to be a mom, and how badly George wanted to be a dad, and he provided. God never lets us down. The lessons we learn along the way are not just for ourselves, everything we have is something we must share and by sharing we keep receiving. It's a wonderful cycle. Give and take, give and take…and you always win, God always gives more.

Anna's fever was high and George took the call, And, our first sign of the day was happening. She was limp and crying, and all of a sudden Anna popped up from having this horrible fever of 102 or three and was fine. All better, no sign that she was even sick. Immediately I knew what God was doing, I knew he was showing us that he had it, that he had control over the situation and that we need not worry. We waited a little while to make sure Anna was OK, then we got in the car and drove to my mom and dad's house. It Was really hard to see my mom pretty much in shock. She was always the uplifting positive thinking go-getter kind of person. Her good friend Marie and her husband Don were there. My sisters, Chris and Jane were there too. We all were there staring at one another in shock. Anna broke the silence when she walked over to my mom and said, "the prophet says God delivers speedily" we all just sort of sat there and looked at each other like did she just say that? Three year old's don't say stuff like that. But Mom knew what God was up to. We have to be like a child, and have childlike faith. Let the children come to me. Don't push them away as if they don't matter. You never know what Jesus is going to look like when He brings help and comfort. This message did comfort her peace at least for the moment. God gives us what we need when we need it. It's so hard for adults to have childlike faith.

Almost every day Anna had something to say. God was giving us so many signs. The first day after we had found out, my sister and I were driving to my mom and dads, and we were sort of arguing. Releasing some tension like we do. It was almost dark and two blackbirds were wrestling up in the air, fighting like crazy and suddenly crashed into our windshield, got tossed behind us and died. We took that as a sign from God that he didn't want us fighting. Of course, we weren't quite done with our "discussion" when we pulled up to a stop sign later on our way home when we saw a bird sitting on the stop sign. I know this might seem lame but the message came through. God was trying to get us to stop bickering. We need to be strong for mom. It was unusual to see birds out after dark. These signs we took because with them we gained knowledge and understanding. God used birds and butterflies a lot.

We spent almost every day with mom. My job was flexible. I had wonderful customers who understood and arranged their schedules to work around all that was going on. George was able to work around his schedule too. My dad had a job he couldn't leave, so it was good my sisters and I and Marie were around. I knew I didn't want to be anywhere else.

The terrible thing with cancer of the pancreas was the incredible pain. Mom battled without pain meds for the most part. She had an allergy to most everything. It especially was bad during the night. I don't think she slept more than two or three hours a night. Maybe a little nap during the day, otherwise we spent most of our time talking and praying the rosary. We would discuss how to trust in God's plan and prayed for His will to be done. We juiced asparagus, and just about everything else. There was no treatment and we knew that was ok. Mom never asked, "Why Me Lord". She was a fighter, and battled in prayer and with holistic medicine. Mom loved being a Grandma and was only 55. None of us were about to let her go. So, we waited...for the daily message or the sign or and sometimes we got both.

For instance, the day I was out for a walk before going to see mom. I went every morning for about an hour with my golden retriever princess. We were coming down a hill and I could see something up ahead about two blocks away. It was a beautiful sunny morning and my eyes were blurry from crying. I had to get it out before going to see her. I didn't want her to see me sad, we couldn't be negative. Anything is possible and we knew that. Remember less than one percent chance of getting Anna? Anyway, my eyes were just fixed on it, but it was pretty far away. What the heck is it. When I got up close, like right up next to it, I couldn't believe what I was seeing. It was a bird, sitting on the sidewalk. This was very strange, it was about 7:30 AM when most birds are out flying around and this little bird was sitting ever so peacefully in the middle of the sidewalk. Here I am 5 inches away from it which in itself is a miracle because I'm afraid of birds, "A" and with a golden retriever who retrieves birds, "B" and this bird had its head tucked underneath it's wing sound asleep. The message that came to me was be at peace, have no fear. When I got home, which was about three blocks away I couldn't wait to tell George. He jumped in his truck and went down the street and sure enough it was still sitting there. When he got home he said, "Yeah, I saw it, but the funny thing is, a man was walking up the hill and walked right past it and didn't even notice it!" This same bird I saw almost 2 blocks before I got to it. That's because that bird was meant for me to see. For years, I would take this walk and pray and listen to the birds and grow closer to God, I would ask God to help me see all of the things he wants me to see to hear all of the things he wants me to hear to share all the things he wants me to share. I prayed that prayer for many years.

Later in the day, we were visiting with mom, Anna brought me over this white dove music box that was sitting on the end table. It was ceramic and sitting on a spring branch. It was pretty and breakable. Of course, I told her not touch it. Instead she brought it over to me. Being a little curious myself, I wound it up to see what the song was. It wasn't what I expected, it played Silent Night. Usually decorations that play silent night look like a Christmas decoration but this didn't. It was just a white bird sitting on Spring branch playing silent night. I felt like it went along with my bird from that morning, to be at peace. Peace is the goal for each day… peace be with you.

Another day, Anna took some holy water that I gotten from my friend Gladys. She had visited a place that the Blessed mother had been appearing and she brought me some holy water. This place attracted thousands of people and many people didn't believe it was true. Nonetheless I was very appreciative of the holy water and was even more in love with the fact that she brought it to me in a cheese whiz jar.

We were on our way out to see mom as usual and when we got there she was up walking around. After a little bit Anna took her hand and said " Nama, why don't you lay down on the couch." Then Anna asked me get two candles and light them both because THIS holy water is real. Sometimes when I tell our stories people think that Anna says these things because she hears me say them, but I can honestly tell you that I've never said things like this before and she didn't even know that I had Holy water and she didn't even know what holy water was. She is three. All that this meant to me at that very moment, was that we don't have to worry about whether or not the Blessed mother had been appearing, this holy water was real. We did what she said, we lit the candles she took her tiny little hand and dipped it into the cheese whiz jar and started making the sign of the cross on Nama. While she was making the sign of the cross on my mom's abdomen and her heart and her for head she was saying a little prayer. She said, "Dear Lord, thank you for Jesus, thank you for the Blessed Mother, thank you for the Holy Spirit, thank you for the rainbows thank you for the birds thank you for the butterflies amen." Then she told my mom to forgive her brother. I didn't know what that meant and later on finally I got it out of my mom that her brother had told her that he would never love her because it was her fault that their mother died. She probably never thought too much about it. Her relationship with her brothers was good. Forgiveness is such a huge part of healing. More signs that the Lord was fully aware and present with Mom. The birds and the butterflies and all of what Anna was saying was a lesson for us to just be thankful. We had been shown many signs where God had used all of those things. Growing up I heard my mother say 1 million times you only need to ask God once he already knows your needs after you've asked him you thank him because his answer is coming. So, thank you Jesus for using Anna to help us remember to be thankful and forgiving.

Another time, we were sitting in my living room, it was a beautiful day, and I was thankful that mom had gotten out of the house for a while. I'm sure she was thankful too. All of us were sitting around. my sisters, my dad, George and I with mom in the living room praying the rosary. Suddenly, Anna says "I have something to say!" Of Course, we all stop what we were doing to listen. She said "1954" actually it was nineteen ifty four. We looked at each other with confusion on our faces and I said, "what happened in 1954?" She said, "that's the year daddy was born." I looked at George and said, "you were born in 1954?" He said, "well no,1955." I thought to myself well she's real close I wasn't even sure what year he was born. Later on, after we finished our rosary I asked her how she knew what year daddy was born and she said, "when did Grandma Bunny die anyway?" I thought to myself, Grandma Bunny, George's mom was trying to let us know that she was present with us and praying with us and helping us get through these hard times. I had never met Bunny, but I know she would've been there to help in any way she could. There's so much going on in the unseen world. We forget that our angels and especially our guardian Angel never leave us. The room was filled with love. This journey was really something for all of us.

Another time we were praying the rosary in my mom and dad's living room, when my sisters Rosary turned gold!! Another confirmation of all of the teachings we learned about but never dreamed would actually happen. Mom used to say "you don't have to travel across the world to receive a miracle, a miracle can happen in your own living room. They happen every day kids"… she used to say....

Fr. Terra has a place in our hearts too. He was from California and had lived with my Uncle Jim and Aunt Mary Kay for a little while in Santa Barbara. My mom had called Uncle Jim to ask him whatever happened to Father Terra. He was a healing priest that would pray over people and they would be healed. Mom thought it would be a good thing to get ahold of him. Uncle Jim thought that was a great idea but they had lost contact with him. He thought Fr. Terra might be living in Yucca Valley. They were going to be going to a wedding in LA and will leave early to go and try and connect with him. It was a good thing that they left early because they had gotten the time wrong on the wedding and it turned out that they made it to the wedding just in time. God doesn't miss a beat. A wonderful surprise happened on the way back from communion. Wouldn't you know it? Fr. Terra was there at the wedding mass!! He was a guest also. They sat together at the reception and yes, Father Terra had remembered my mom. She had written him a few letters years before asking him to pray for us so that we may have a baby. Maybe it was his praying that helped orchestrate nurse Judy talking to Jeanne?? Anyway, he and Father Joe had left their parish and had begun a ministry of healing masses around the country. He sent my mom his schedule and the closest he was going to be was a 10-hour Drive to Manitowoc Wisconsin. The miracle of this was the letter from father Terra came to my mom with no address and no ZIP Code! Just her name, all the way from Yucca Valley California and was received into our mailbox in two days. I don't know maybe you think I'm stretching it but I think that's a miracle. It's hard to get mail that fast even with an address!!! Uncle Jerry, my mom's other brother got us a van and we hauled my mom in the back of the van 10 hours to the healing mass. This was a very long ride. Mom had to take pain meds in order to make the trip. I felt like that story in the bible where the friends were trying to get their sick friend to see Jesus so they cut a hole in the roof and lowered him down. A very desperate time. We all were prayed over. Mom felt a ping when she was being prayed over.

But the pain was very severe and was not going away. All summer long when I asked her where she wanted to go after she was healed she would say Door County. It was one of her happy places to be. Oddly, Door County is only an hour away from Manitowoc Wisconsin. So, we made the drive up and spent three days there. It was kind of like torture, she was in extreme pain and it wasn't fun at all. She could not eat and hadn't slept for a very long time but she never stopped believing, she battled. We got back in the van and decided to drive home. All of our prayers we continued, we never stopped, we never gave up, we gathered all the saints and all the angels healing angels, everyone we could think of in heaven to help us pray. We were almost home and driving down Rose Street about 30 miles from town when all of a sudden, her pain left, it went away!! Here we are on Rose Street!! Some might call that a coincidence, but I don't believe in them. This was such great miracle. It was a marvelous to see my mom's coloring come back and look like herself again. You see, not only was her cancer in her pancreas it was also in her liver. From the very beginning, there was no treatment or anything that could be done to help. We used naturopathic and it did give her relief but this journey was still not over. Speaking of naturopathic, the healing plant for the pancreas is the iris. For 10 years at least, my mom had a photograph of a purple iris on her desk at work, that had the image of Christ in the pedal. It wasn't until after we found out she had cancer that we noticed there was an image of Satan at the top of the flower. Freaky! It was a real photograph, there was no photo shopping back then. This came with a message for me and that is: God doesn't want us sick and doesn't give us things like illness to test us or punish us. Illness somehow comes from evil and it delights in making us sick. Not sure how the devil makes it happen but my idea is stress and worry. Just an idea and who knows right?

The one thing my mom said from the very beginning was that she was going to flush this cancer down the toilet. She had an Aunt Rose that had cancer when she was 42 and was still alive...she was 92 years old. I guess not everybody died super young in her family. Aunt Rose always talked about flushing her cancer down the toilet. Sadly, that was the hardest thing at that moment for her to do. You see the two days that she spent taking pain medication, turned her gut into cement. She was having a really hard time. Her stomach was beginning to distend and it was very uncomfortable. She no longer had the pain that she had before she was prayed over, but she just couldn't get it to move. We took her into the emergency room where they tapped your stomach to remove the fluid. The doctor had come to us and said that he imagined that the fluid would be full of cancer cells. "It always is" he said. We asked him not to say anything to her because we had just come from a healing mass and she was so much better her pain was all gone. He looked at us quite sympathetically and a little bit like he pitied us. I asked him when he would find out the results of the tests on the fluid and he said it would be three days. The next morning the phone rang real early, it was mom, crying, she rarely cried. I asked her what happened and she said the doctor had come in and told her that he thought the fluid would be full of cancer cells. I told her this might not be true he said he won't find out for three days. We had been to a healing mass. He doesn't understand. She said, "that's not why am crying Jo, I'm crying because we've already received a miracle for the day! Our angel came into my room this morning at 6:30. This little old lady came in to empty the garbage and asked me why I was in there. I told her about the cancer and she said, oh honey, I don't want you to worry about that, I had cancer too but I was healed at a healing mass." Mom was so excited her tears were happy tears. She knew that lady was an angel. She could've said that she had surgery and many rounds of chemo and radiation. But she said a healing mass. She wanted mom to know she was healed. Claiming your miracle can be the hardest part. Besides, I don't think it's common for someone to come in to take out your garbage at 6:30 in the morning. We knew this was another messenger from our Lord. They always seem to have a special "way" about them. It would be just like the lord to come as someone emptying the garbage. Love Him

We got her out of the hospital and in a few days her stomach started to fill again, she still had not gone to the bathroom yet. We took her down to mayo clinic this time to have her stomach tapped again. Even though you have hope and you know that God is taking care of everything, you still get a sick feeling in your stomach. I even had a feeling of despair at times. I could see it on mom's face too. While my mom was in with the doctor I peeked my head in the door to sit with her for a while. The Doc had stepped out so she was sitting alone and was glad to have me sit with her. She said that she had taken a peek at the file and the fluid was negative. Remember this is the fluid that we were told would be full of cancer cells…it always is? Our real issue was that because she was terminal, there wasn't anything they could do or planned on doing. Like a colostomy, why not? They didn't understand a healing mass I guess. Mom said "Jo, it's negative we just got to get it out of me."

It was so hard those next couple of weeks because she was in tremendous pain from the blockage. We didn't stop praying, Anna kept giving us little bits of wisdom like… Nama don't worry, you are healed, and forgive Grandma Morgan. She was the Aunt that mom lived with. God didn't stop showing us His amazing grace and mercy.

Dad, Chris and Jane took Mom to the emergency room on a Sunday night, in the middle of October. The weather was unusually warm and summer like. It had been a cool and rainy summer and that was unusual for us. Mom said it was perfect because she loved the rain. I still have a clear picture in my mind of Anna giving her Nama a big hug as we helped Mom out of the house. Anna was her only grandchild so far, and they were always hugging. She had a hard time letting go of Nama this time and the same for Mom. George was also struggling. He and my mom were so close. Much of his time all summer, he spent lying with mom just talking. I think she would talk to him about dying, he had been through it with his mother. We wouldn't allow any negative talk but I know George let mom talk about everything. Mother, I hope you can forgive me for not letting you talk about the things you needed to. Please forgive me for being so selfish.

This was her Holy week. On Monday, she was in the hospital and my sisters and my dad were with her, I was working that day and thankfully I was. I had a customer give me a phone number of a man from Wisconsin who prayed for people. His name was Norman. I asked for his phone number and immediately called him that afternoon. We had a nice long talk and he was telling me about all the people he prayed for that were healed. Two with brain tumors just that day had called him to tell him about their healing. I had told him about the healing she already experienced but he said sometimes you need extra prayers for other things that come up. Mom was a little bit upset at the very beginning of the week because they had given her morphine right when she got to the emergency room. She told them she didn't have any pain that she just needed to poop. They said, "what are you talking about you have pancreatic cancer!" and I gave her the medicine. So of course, that made it worse for her, what she needed was a colostomy. She was from the era where you never question your medical doctor and in most cases, that's ok but in some situations, we need to ask a lot of questions and talk things out. She reacted pretty violently to the morphine and they didn't give her anymore. I told her about Norman and that he was praying for her.

On Tuesday morning Marie was with me and we had to leave the room for them to draw some blood and do some test so we went to the cafeteria. The cafeteria was packed with people, no place to sit. This was unusual, normally it was empty, I had to ask a man if we could sit at his table. He said sure, so we sat there for 15 minutes and didn't talk at all. When we got up to leave, I looked at this man and thanked him for sharing his table. He looked right into my eyes, he had crystal clear blue eyes, and he looked right into me… and said, "you're a believer, aren't you?" I said, "yes I am" and he said "there is something you need to know. Your mother's love ones on the other side are pulling just as hard to get her there as you are to keep her here." I thanked him for the message and I turned to walk away. I was thankful that I didn't punch him. If this was true, then we have no chance. There are so many loved ones on the other side. We walked a few feet when Marie said to me "that was an angel" I said "yeah I know." We got back to mom's room and I didn't even tell her about the angel in the cafeteria. I didn't want her to give up and didn't want her to think about the other side. I wanted her to stay with us, she's only 55 years old, she's only been a grandma for three years, it wasn't time. My selfishness was driving my fear. Or maybe it's the other way around.

On Wednesday of her holy week she started talking about Easter which had us all a little confused, but we were trying to stay positive with that big huge pit in our stomachs. We continued to pray the rosary almost nonstop. George stayed home with Anna while I would go to the hospital. The picture I can't stop thinking about is the great big hug that Anna gave Nama on Sunday night before she left for the hospital. Was Anna going to get to see her Nama again? Must've been so hard for mom, to be so positive and battle so hard. When we walk by faith we always have hope. Now it's Wednesday in the afternoon she was sitting on the side of the bed and rocking back-and-forth in a lot of pain. All of a sudden, she just stopped and looked at me and said, "oh my gosh." I said, "what mom." She said "I can hear him praying, I can hear Norman praying for me. I can hear everything he is saying to me. It's as if he were sitting right here next to me!" Oh my gosh, all I could think was how close she must be. How hard it must be for her to stay. It's one of those miracles that happened again to show us how very small we really are, and how little we have control over. It shows once again, that in the unseen world so much is going on. In this world, our heavy bodies keep us blinded. God can't show us everything. We wouldn't want to stay here and live our mission or serve our purpose. She was close to being out of her body her spirit was so strong and so ready, and I'm just really thankful that I was there to hear her explain what that was like to be able to hear someone praying for her. It shows that our prayers are heard as if we were sitting right next to the person we are praying for or with. When we call out their names, Jesus, Blessed Mother, Saint Theresa, Saint Jude, Saint Michael, any one of them... Not to mention the Angels they are there!! When we but whisper their name, they are there to come to our aid. When we pray for others we send angels hundreds of angels to help them. Our prayers are so powerful, and they are our greatest gift, they are how we communicate with our Lord and how we communicate with our loved ones. Never doubt the power of your prayers.

Now it's Thursday. And I have to be honest this story one of the harder ones I have to tell. Thursday was really a Holy Thursday for my mom. It seemed as if the room was getting darker and darker as the week went on. I kept thinking are there no lights? Why is it so dark in here? Mom just sat on the side of the bed in a lot of pain and her voice was barely audible. They were giving her fluid pills and it was drying out her whole body. There was only one time when she said, "What is the Lord doing? Even Jesus only suffered for a few hours." Then, she took it back and said she understood what His suffering was about and knew He was the teacher. We suffer through things to unite ourselves to Christ. She was always a teacher too.

The weather outside was beautiful. The fall trees were gorgeous and the temperature was still unseasonably warm. I was going home late at night to see Anna and George. My sisters and I drove together and all I remember is praying the rosary. Over and over again. It brought us peace. We still had hope that they could get her to go potty but they weren't really talking about it much. I kept thinking why can't they just do a colostomy.

Thursday was another day of waiting... During the evening

mom and I were alone in the room. Some relatives had come to the hospital and were visiting down the hall in the family area. I was rubbing moms back when all of the sudden she got startled and her eyes got huge. She didn't move and did not look away from whatever it was. I have seen this look before in a movie about apparitions. Places the blessed mother would appear. It's a look of ecstasy. She whispered to me that He was here! He was here!! I asked, "who? Mom who is here?" She said, "the bible, the bible is here!" I told her that we forgot to even bring her bible. "NO!! HE'S HERE!!" She never blinked or looked away and I said, "you mean Jesus? Jesus is here?" She said, "yes!!" I said, "Well what does he want??" She said, "He wants to talk to me. I told her I wasn't going to leave the room because she'll leave with him. She promised she wouldn't, but he wants to talk to her.

It was all I could do to leave her alone with him. You see we had been to many, many, funerals and usually the person who died, would pass away when the family left the room. It is our theory that we hold them here and we have to let go so they can be with the lord. She knew what I was thinking and promised. Seriously the most selfish thing I've ever done so far in this lifetime.

When I got back to the room she was back to normal, but had a sad look on her face. She was battling to live and continue her job as mother, wife and grandmother. She had so much left to give. She looked at me with sad eyes and said, "He wants me up there." I know deep down she was very ready. She had so much love waiting for her up there. But I also know she didn't want to leave us. It was the first moment that we realized she wasn't going to get to stay. This whole long week, we had figured they would figure out a way for her to go. I looked back at her, both of us with sad eyes, and said, "Well mom you'd better go then. We can't argue with Jesus." She didn't go that night. She went through the most excruciatingly long and painful night. My sister Jane and my Dad stayed with her and I went home so George could come be with her early Friday morning. Pretty sure she cut a deal with the lord. She wanted to have the colostomy they had planned for Friday. The pain was so bad, they had to strap her down to wheel her to surgery. She couldn't lie flat. I got there before she left for surgery, George and I prayed over her like we had done so many times, we all felt so helpless. I called Norman to help pray along with the many prayer chains going across the country. This is my mom!! Lord take care of her. While I was talking to Norman he had to hang up because he said my mom needed him right now. The nurse came running down the hall needing to talk to my dad. The issue was that she was so impacted that the surgeons were afraid if they opened her up she would explode all over. But if they don't do the surgery, she will be in this horrible pain for another week. My dad said we have to do something. A few hours later the docs were back and they said miraculously what they thought would happen didn't. But that it was all over her. There was no more they can do. We spent the rest of Friday and all-day Saturday with her. She never woke up and really didn't even look sick. She looked beautiful and was glowing. She gave us time to just be with her but I think she was in and out of heaven that whole time. When my sisters and I finally left her late Saturday night, we just said see us later Momma. We told her we would be watching and listening for all the signs and wonders she and Jesus and the Blessed Mother and all our loved ones will have for us. We have to leave Mom because we don't want to hold you here. My dad stayed with her. The next morning, Sunday at 5:17 Anna woke up crying. I ran up the stairs, she usually doesn't cry. When I got up there she was fast asleep. Kind of weird. That's when I thought to look at the time. A couple of hours later my dad called me. He was crying... He said she did it!! She is there!! I asked him what time dad? He said 5:17. Yea she must have stopped by to say goodbye to Anna. Easter was her favorite and her Easter had come. I went to take a shower and cried until I thought I might pass out. I yelled at God and asked him what the heck? All those miracles?? Then that smell came over me. It had happened one other time. It was very distinct. I searched all over the bathroom for potpourri or something with that smell. But nothing. Later in the month, I realized what it was. It was frankenscense. The smell of insense that is at every special mass, it was Jesus comforting me. God answered me and said all the signs and miracles were spiritual. Mom received her healing and everything Anna said, all the healing that took place was spiritual. He didn't want her to suffer any longer. Her physical body had been healed too but she was ready to go. These were the thoughts that came to me and I felt peace. That day was something. All day lots of people came over to visit and every single one Anna greeted and exclaimed that her Nama got to go to heaven today. She was so excited for her Nama. Now we have to figure out how to live without her physically with us. We know she is with us every time we but whisper her name. It's been 23 years almost to the day as I'm writing this and it still makes me cry. She was so special and so missed every day. Thank you, Jesus, for being with us and for giving me such a great mom.

Acts 2:28 *You have made known to me the paths of life: you will fill me with joy in your presence.'*

# Jackee

The time after mom passed away seemed to go by very slowly. I remember feeling like every day was dark. I even called Norman and asked him why God had left me. He said "O honey, you feel like you can't hear His voice because your heart is so heavy. But these are the times He really carries you. That made sense to me and eventually the days got sunnier.

Anna continued to say interesting things and we continued to listen. One day in- particular Anna was sure we needed to go to Carter's to shop. She was four and didn't care much for shopping. I asked her what the big deal was... She said we needed to get outfits for her baby sister. "She is coming in July Mom" she said. I was excited to hear this news because like I told you before it was less than one percent chance to get our first child and ZERO percent to get our second one. Being the prayers warriors that we are we didn't doubt. It's easy to doubt when they give you no hope. This was about one year after mom had passed and she always said more could be done from heaven than we ever could on earth. So, our prayers were not just our comfort but our tool and weapon against any doubts. I wasn't sure right away how to handle our shopping for outfits but decided to show God our confidence in him by going ahead and picking out two things. Both for summertime. Anna of course was a little annoyed when I asked her what year this would happen. She didn't know.

The following summer, we decided to take a few days and

head out of town for a little rest and relaxation. It was very hot and swimming in a big pool sounded fun. We drove for two hours to this really "cool pool" and were so excited. The day was July 6<sup>th</sup>, 1994. It was my grandpa Roy's birthday and I found myself very weepy. I cried on and off thru the whole drive and told George that I wasn't sure what was going on but it was big. I thought maybe I was missing my grandpa. He passed away in my backyard when I was 8. He had a heart attack while riding on the snowmobile. It was a long dark day that day too. A blizzard was going on and the ambulance took over two hours to get to our house. It seemed odd that I would be crying so many years later but with me ... Who knows.

Anyway, we get to the marvelous pool and the lifeguards had just gotten off their stands for their break. About five minutes later they went back into the pool in a long straight line inspecting the bottom of the pool. Sure enough they found poop and closed the pool. Haha, funny stuff, you can't make this up, right? We drive two hours didn't even get our toes wet and, yea that was that. Don't you wonder how George does it? Then, of course, a terrible storm blew in and we decided to go to the movie or go home. The lion king was coming out that very day. Perfect. So, we went to the movie, the rain didn't stop for two days and then we drove home. Fun times.

Interesting things happened during that week. I cried all day on the sixth and didn't know why remember. When we got home on that Weekend we went to church on Sunday as usual. After mass, we went to Wimpy's for breakfast. We went every week and they pretty much knew our order and had it ready when we got there. They would say "Anna!!" When we walked in. On this particular day July 9<sup>th</sup>,1994 our beautiful Jackee had just gotten a job there, it was her first day. She was one of our babysitters that lived down the street. She and her best friend Jessie would come over to hang out with Anna and visit with me. Jackee had moved to the country and I hadn't seen her in a few weeks. I was so happy and excited to see her. She was fifteen and easily embarrassed. So, I did my thing. As we left the restaurant I backed out of the place blowing her kisses and hollering that I loved her and that I promised to never forget her birthday. George, Anna and I got out to the sidewalk and I stopped and just stared at her. She was glowing. I told George to look... She was glowing and he said, "Wow, she is! She is glowing." That's how I left her blowing kisses and telling her I loved her.

The next morning very early, I got a phone call from her mom that Jackee had been killed in a car accident. Oh, my lord no!!! Her mom and I cried for a while on the phone and the only thing that came to me to say to her, was that I had seen Jackee the day before and she was glowing. It was as if her spirit knew she was on her way to heaven and her excitement couldn't be contained. She had been hit by a train and thrown from the car. I hung up the phone is sheer disbelief and cried and cried. Jackee was like my baby sister. Anna came over to me to ask what was wrong. I told her what happened and she looked at me with a happy, excited face and said, "momma it was her day!!" I knew that was the truth but I said to Anna, "honey, I'm not sad for her I'm said for me and for her family" she thought that seemed logical. Then a few minutes later she walked over to me to tell me that Nama loves butterflies....

The same day my brother in-law, Paul went to the cemetery to just have some quiet time. His first wife was buried really close to my Mom's grave. He called me to tell me about the strange thing that happened to him while there. A big monarch butterfly bumped him in the forehead then fluttered over to my Mom's headstone and sat there for a while. He said it didn't flutter away, but rather it bolted right straight up and out of sight. (People know it's safe to tell me about the weird things that happen to them.) He thought that was pretty weird. I said something even weirder happened, Anna told me this morning that Nama loves butterflies. We took it as a sign as her way of letting us know she is around to comfort us in our grief. Jackee's friends all came over to my house that evening to talk and cry. Jessie was really hurting. They were inseparable. As we chatted Jessie said that Jackee always wanted to have about 17 kids. I thought really wow!! I never knew that, I thought I knew everything about Jackee but I came to me that she wouldn't say something like that to me because she wouldn't want to hurt my feelings with having infertility. She was that kind. But looking around the room and counted her close friends and classmates there was a total of 17 in her class. A very small class that year. She was just 15. She was so faith-filled and close to the Lord. So beautiful.

> Romans 12:2 *Do not conform yourselves to this age but be transformed by the renewal of your mind, that you may discern what is the will of God, what is good and pleasing and perfect.*

# Prayers with the Moms

Something else happened that day too. That Sunday after we went to Wimpy's, my dad came over to share some exciting news. He had many years before wanted to buy a greenhouse business and was about a week away from sealing the deal when a man named Dick Donahue bought it. So, when Dad sat George down to tell him the great news that Dick was selling the mum portion of the business, George and Dad talked for a minute and George decided to give Dick a call. The funny part of this story is that the night before I had said a prayer to George's Mom, my Mom and the Blessed Mother and asked them to intercede for George. He needed a different job. He was really good in sales. My mom had been his secretary and for the last two years since she passed he lost his zeal for it. The insurance business did him well. We got a few good trips out of it. He reached the top fifty agents in the nation but was done. Life is too short I told the moms. I also laughed a little while praying because it was midnight and I was going potty. (I always told my confirmation kids to pray while they pee it makes good use of their time). The second funny thing, I joked that I'm asking the women for help because women get things done fast. Jesus can't say no to the moms. So, when dad came, the very next morning, all excited it shouldn't have surprised me.

George picked up the phone to call Dick and the phone rang in his hand. It was Dick. He had some insurance questions and then he and George talked about the mums. George hung up the phone and looked at me and said, "well what do you think?" I said, "I think we should do it!!" He said "just like that? I don't know anything about it!!" I said, "I know but I prayed last night to your mum, my mum, and the blessed mum and they brought us mums!" Ha well that's all it took for George. He looked at my dad and his excitement and went for it. Dad and George made plans to have it out on my dad's property. Lots had to be done. My dad was coming up on retirement and this was the perfect thing to occupy him. God's timing. It was something he always wanted. George said he was happy that he got to work with my mom and now he would get to work with my dad. It's one of those things that if you knew how much hard work it was going to take and how impossible it seemed you would never do it. George worked 7 days a week and paid himself nothing for the first three years. Yet God provided. My hair business was busy and he had some residual checks but when I tell people he didn't pay himself for three years they don't believe me. People who have started a business believe me. You have to have a pioneer spirit and depend on God. We put a statue of the blessed mother in all the greenhouses and she reminds us to stay in prayer. We are thankful for her protection as well, there have been a few times when straight-line winds have taken trees out on both sides of the greenhouses and our stuff was untouched. A couple of tornados have suddenly changed courses over the years too. Love her!!

John 15:5 *I am the vine, you are the branches. Whoever remains in me and I in him will bear much fruit, because without me you can do nothing.*

# Baby Girl Laura

It's September 1994 and our world got a little wild after deciding to start our brand-new business. George spent long nights reading everything he could get his hands on. I was trying to work as much as possible to keep groceries on the table in the meantime. Of course, we weren't too worried, God continued to provide. We just had to do our part and not want stuff. Our needs were being taken care of.

It was the first day of kindergarten for Anna and way too much for me to handle. I couldn't even believe she was going to be gone all day every day. We had done preschool where she was queen of the recycling table but this was different. I still have etched in my mind the picture of her little hand waving me off with her white blonde hair glowing in the morning sunshine. She was fine, she was ready, real independent and … I cried most of the day. Something most mothers can relate to I'm sure but when it's happening to you... It's worse. I went out to the greenhouse that wasn't even a greenhouse yet, it was just a spot of land. George's dad "Poopsie" was there giving me a hard time as usual. I was letting George know that he would have to pick Anna up from school on Thursday because I had to work. He said that would be fine. Poopsie was curious as to why I was worrying about Thursday?? It's only Tuesday!! I said "well what's in the way? Wednesday?" We laughed and didn't think too much of the conversation. Anna had a great first day of school and couldn't wait for the second day…

Wednesday!! I dropped Anna off and went to church. Had to have a little talk with Jesus. I was crying, silently at least, but Jesus had to listen to my whining. Really Lord? I can't believe just one child for us. You have to fix me I'm a mess!! I don't have time to be here Jesus. I have to go to the dentist, go get groceries then go to work. Hurry up and fix me! I need your help. Blessed Mother, Mom please pray for me. Oh, and saint Theresa too and I listed a long list of my saint friends that are used to hearing from me. I felt so much better and knew that I would get through this feeling of loneliness. I'm never really alone anyway.

A few short hours later, after the dentist and groceries but before work. A knock came to the door. It was Carol our most recent social worker that updated our study after we had Anna. She had that look on her face and I was already stunned before she even opened her mouth. She stood in my back door and asked where is George? I told her we might not be able to get ahold of him because we were starting a new business and he wouldn't be near a phone. (No cell phones) oddly I called the number and he answered!! Come home I said we have big news. In just a few minutes George was there and we were given the wonderful news of our little baby girl!!! Amazing!!! Anna's little sister that she seemed to know all about!! We went to school to pick her up and were so excited to tell her the news. She was excited but more relieved. She was finally going to see the sister she was waiting for. And guess what? You guessed it!! Our baby was being born on that very day that I was crying all day. The same day as my grandpa Roys birthday. We had so little time to get ready but that didn't matter. Our hearts were ready!!! News traveled fast and once again people came to help us get everything we needed. We prayed every day and night for so long. When someone tells you it's impossible, pray anyway.

It turns out that Wednesday that was in between Tuesday and Thursday was big!! I didn't have to worry about picking up Anna from school. I started my mommy time off that Wednesday after groceries the dentist and work. God managed to provide for us. And worrying two days ahead was useless. God is so good at teaching us and bringing the gospel to life. Something I always prayed for was for God to bless us with another child and to have it be with just as many miracles surrounding us. I needed our second baby to know how special Gods plan was for her life too. It is God's plan for every life to be received as a miracle. We receive Jesus with every life and it is so overwhelming to receive that much love. Of course, there is more to this story.

We drove in the pouring rain the day we went to get our baby Laura. It was raining so hard that we had to pull over to wait it out. Sitting in the car, in the pouring rain, (did I mention it was raining?) out in the middle of nowhere, we noticed an abandoned shed with great big letters on the side of it. R O Y. It's crazy and wonderful how heaven can communicate with us if we open ourselves to the signs. That was my grandpas name remember? Laura was born on his birthday!?! And, he was the one who died in my backyard when I was eight? We had a special connection and he was letting me know that he was thankful for all the prayers I had prayed for him. At least that was the thought that came to me. One more thing... When we arrived at the home where Laura was being cared for...the first thing we did was to take her picture. She was lying in a little crib by the door. After having the picture developed it had a white cloud on top of her. You could see everything in the picture perfectly except her tiny body was covered in a white haze. God was covering her with his protective Angels. God answers prayers sometimes with such amazing beauty and shows us without a doubt that His plan is worth believing and trusting and waiting for. Thank you, Jesus, for our baby Laura that we love so much.

Thank you, Mom, and the Blessed Mom and all our loved ones in heaven who did more from heaven than ever could have on this earth. Prayers are powerful and so appreciated!

So, the day we went to the "cool pool" was the day Laura was being born. I was crying because my soul knew, just like little Anna knew her baby sister was coming in July. Just like I knew something was happening the day Anna was being born too. I want to add this not because I think I have something special, but because God makes something special for each baby He creates. My girls are all grown up now. They are beautiful, talented, smart, funny and so many other things for George and me for our family, for their future families and for the world. The signs and wonders never cease, they continue to make me a better person and I pray every day in thanksgiving. I also pray every day for all the parents who are without a child. Be with them Lord and give them courage to persevere. Amen

1 Timothy 1:14 *Indeed, the grace of our Lord has been abundant, along with the faith and love that are in Christ Jesus*

# *Butterflies*

Geno and my dad were best friends since they were eight years old. They had a hobby in their childhood that they kept, or shall I say, "obsessed over" forever. They raised pigeons. Don't laugh... I don't get it but my dad still has his birds and now he has gone from show birds to racing pigeons. They get dropped off hundreds of miles from home and make it back before sundown. He and Geno spent all their growing up years together. Geno and his wife Esther were Godparents to my older sister, Chris and so our families have been intertwined for a real long time. In May of 1992, Geno passed away from a long struggle with diabetes. He went through years of dialysis before having a kidney transplant. He had both legs amputated and eventually went blind. All the while he and my dad stayed very close. Dad would keep him laughing or was it the other way around. Geno died in May and my mom got sick in June so in five months they both were gone. Both in their fifties.

Dad and Esther grieved together and in two years or maybe three they were married. After they decided to get married dad wanted to stay in the country...with his birds. My sisters and I worked hard to get the house ready for Esther. Dad pretty much wanted everything out so he decided to have an auction. This wasn't easy for us. Going through Mom's stuff to make the house look like a whole different place. We took the things that my sisters and I wanted to maybe keep to my Chris' basement. We wanted to go through it calmly and respectfully. It was mostly sentimental. My dad was not real understanding of this, but he didn't really have a choice. He wanted everything gone. We all grieve differently and we knew what his motivation was. His heart is always in the right place.

The day came when we were to go through all the stuff... A day we all dreaded. It was just stuff and it really didn't matter it didn't bring her back but we had to do it. When I got to Chris' house I was so surprised and utterly astonished!!! There were millions of monarchs in her yard and all the way down the block!!! Was I in a national geographic episode of the migration of the monarch?? They were draped in every tree and hanging to the ground. Millions and millions not kidding!! This is not something that has ever happened before or since, it was for us for that night, that we once again were given a wonderful sign that Mom was not too far away. That heaven isn't too far away and that Mom and Geno were happy for my Dad and Esther.

Thank you, Jesus, you really are amazing Grace.

> Ecclesiastes 3:11 *God has made everything appropriate to its time, but has put the timeless into their hearts so they cannot find out from the beginning to end, the work which God has done.*

# Confirmation class

So, it one of those deals that you feel like volunteering is a way to show God how much you appreciate Him. In no time, He goes and out gives you once again. There is nothing we can do for the Lord that goes unrewarded.

For many years, I've been a confirmation teacher. Like 33, with a year off every now and then. I'm having an off year this year and I feel off. I was called into this ministry as only God can call. I went kicking and screaming. I remember thinking about it and then going to church only to have them pleading for someone to step up. They are in need of teachers. This is weird, I was just thinking I should do this but I know I'm not qualified to be a teacher. You can't mean me Lord. So, I put it off and the next week same thing, please consider being a teacher, the Holy Spirit will provide you with all you'll need. Oh, ok I'm not required to know everything, I just have to be open to the Holy Spirit. I had to finally surrender so God would let me sleep. Kind of like right now, it's 2:45 am and I'm writing, trying to ignore my thoughts night after night is feudal. So when people say they have a calling, it's really a nagging that happens that won't go away until you surrender to His will.

My world was never the same again after my first class. I could not believe how easy it was to share my faith and love these brothers and sisters of mine. What a privilege to know these people who to this day I call my kids. I remember asking God one day why do I need to keep doing this? does He still want me to be a teacher. Can't I have my Wednesday nights back? Aren't I getting a little too old? Loud and clear in my thoughts I heard "JODIE!! I never let you have a baby come from you but you've been there for the rebirth of so many of my children!!" O!! Ok, He made me cry and I had a flash of all the retreats where I witnessed the Holy Spirit at work. How often I felt like the midwife wiping their tears and holding them, Gods kids, in my arms. He also made it clear to me that all people respond to love. The age of a person is not important but it's the love that connects people. So, I guess it's just what the Lord has given me to do and because of it Lots of little miracles happened even during class. I would love to share some with you for you see if I had a nickel for every time I heard why don't these things happen to me? Or, you should write a book!! I'd be, well I'd have quite a few dollars. I sometimes think my ninth graders are the reason for my heightened awareness. I've always been like this but God really opened me up spiritually and made me aware of all the little things He does for us every day. I think because He knows I'll share it. He doesn't let me miss what He is trying to show me. My prayer life has been such a big part of it all. In prayer, which is really just conversation with God in your heart, I remember asking God to not let me miss a thing. I wanted to see Him more clearly follow Him more nearly, and love Him more dearly day by day (it's a song) and it was through prayer that I was able to grow. All forms, and there are many, are ok and praying unceasingly seems impossible but it really isn't. Pray before you do anything and you will live in joy. Consecrate your heart to the Lord and ask for help in all things. He created us all with a little hole in our hearts that was meant just for Him. We sometimes try and fill that hole with other things, fame, fortune, drugs, alcohol, lots and lots of things. Satan will try and distract us from our true selves, that inner being that belongs only God, our heart and soul.

The blessed mother, our mother, has been appearing around

the world, she reminds us to pray like any mother would. She continues to bring us to her son. Her message is for fasting and prayer because the battle against Satan is real and Our weapon is prayer. Here's a good story for you. Anna was five (this one the kids loved) and I just picked her up from a long day at kindergarten. She immediately asked me, mom! Did you know that the world is evil? Big blue eyes in my rear-view mirror... We are all evil but we aren't bad. I wasn't quite sure how to answer so I just asked her to go on.

You know how to get rid of it mom?" I answered, "are you learning this in school?" She looked at me with a side look and said "No, but you wanna know how we get rid of it?" Yes " I answered. "I would like to know that. How do we get rid of evil?" She said," well it's like it's a war and God fights the war for us. You wanna know how God fights a war mom? I answered, "yes I would, how does God fight a war?" She said, "there are no guns God does not use guns!" I asked, "How can God fight a war without using guns?" She said "Well...He just gives us strength to pray more! Can we go get French fries?"

Wow. Ok just like that the conversation was over and mission accomplished. God had more for me to talk about in class. Prayer of any type, praying in silence or with people, or singing with the radio...If you can picture Jesus singing it then I say it's okay. I would tell the kids and think about the songs that you can't picture Jesus singing...best not listen. It can be like poisen.

Here's another one... I was running late for class, Anna was about seven and she didn't want me to leave. Why do you have to go? I told her I wasn't exactly sure but it has to do with sharing Gods love. She said, "come here mom and put your hand on the bible" I said " I really don't have time Anna" it seemed important so I took a minute. I put my hand on the bible and she said, this is a story about a man, a very bad man who never prayed in his whole life. He died and went down, down, into darkness. This is when he said his first prayer: O my God please help me and the

Angels swooped down and grabbed him and carried him up, up, He didn't get to go all the way up but he was happy." That was the end of the story. Just like that she kissed me and told me to have a good night at class. I rushed to the class and was unprepared as usual (I relied heavily on the Holy Spirit) and when all else fails get the book out. I opened the book and for that night the topic was "teach me to pray " oh how perfect!! I had a story for the kids. In case you're wondering why we pray? It's to keep you from going down, down, no biggie.

My challenge to them was why on earth would a person wait until their death bed to pray? Why would we miss out on a life of joy? God gives us gifts and talents and a mission every single day!! Being in prayer is what turns on the light so we don't stumble down the path in the dark. Isn't it better to go into the dark forest with the very person who made the forest? The one who knows the way? He knows what path he wants us on we have only to take His hand and allow Him to guide us! Does this mean we won't make mistakes? No! But He even knows that and will be there to catch us when we fall. My daughter said to me once, "you know mom nobody needs to be perfect. If we think we're perfect then we think we don't need God!" This is true and God loves us more than we could ever know. The only thing He requires of us is to love Him back and invite Him into our lives!! It's so simple and yet humanity struggles with it. Because of the battle and our busy lives that keep us from praying.

Every night in class the kids would say tell us a story tell us a story. Of course, I would say we need to accomplish the night's goals then they would get a story. I used to think and some people would say that people with a weak faith need stories or signs. This sort of confuses me. The whole bible is about stories. Signs and wonders visions and spiritual blessings, and I know there is one place in the bible that Jesus was showing his humanness and exhaustion. I don't know, preaching and feeding five thousand was probably tiring even for God. Even God needed a break and had to go rest under the olive tree. Still the people followed Him wanting more. He became annoyed and asked them to just love him and why must you need more signs. Five loaves and two fish that just fed over five thousand wasn't enough for you to believe? I'm not good at quoting scripture but I think about this in my heart and what Jesus must have felt like. Probably wanted to bang his head on the trunk of the tree. But instead He just loved them. And kept teaching. He came here to show us how to serve. So, when people give me crap about my stories and these people were never the kids, I always think about what Jesus taught. Just love them. Besides why wouldn't God continue to give us signs especially if we ask for them. The people that walked with him physically needed signs why would He love us any less? Ask people!! Ask for God to show Himself to you He never tires because He has given us the gift of Himself through His Holy Spirit. Most of what we are is spiritual. We are hindered by our bodies and even the Lord taught us that he also felt exhaustion in his human body. The lord is shutting my brain down I think it's time for sleep. Ttyl peace

I just remembered another special story from class. All my kids were special but on this particular year I was being challenged by a young man that seemed to hate being there. He was a troubled kid and loved to disrupt the class. He did come every week which I thought was something of a miracle but he was sure battling. Every week the other kids would get frustrated and not very kindly say they wanted me to throw him out in the hall. He didn't seem phased by their unkind reaction but a little surprised with me. I refused to throw him out in the hall because he was my brother and I care for him. I love him. Plus, that's what he wants me to do.

This went on for about five or six meetings and I'll never forget the night it all changed. He had started a fire in school that day and was proud to tell us about it. I ignored it but he was especially naughty that night. The kids were angry with him and it hit the fan. I stopped and asked him what he would like me to do. He said he didn't care. He didn't even believe in God. I said this is why I refuse to discard you because Jesus died on the cross just for you. If you were the only person on the earth He would've done the same thing. He didn't care. I told the kids that instead of throwing him out let's show him some love. They were willing and to my amazement so was he. I laid my hands on him and asked the kids to put their hands on him too. I prayed out loud and the melting began. Jesus and His Holy Spirit covered him and changed all of us. After class, this young man stayed to talk to me and told me what his life was like. His dad was a severe alcoholic and it made life very hard. His mother did all she could but he had never thought God existed. I told him that he wasn't alone EVER and God was dragging him to class to break his heart of stone. I promised him that by the end of our year together he would understand how much he is loved. He would also be able to pray for his dad and his family.

Our confirmation was at the Cathedral in St Paul and it was a very special day for everyone. The kids couldn't wait to tell me that our brother, who had battled all year or at least most of it, was sitting at the very front and would be getting confirmed first!! They were more excited than I was for him. One thing that is so amazing about prayer is that when you pray with or for someone, it bonds you forever. That is what love can do. We think our prayers aren't being heard or don't matter…that would be a huge lie.

A few years later, his sister was in my class and she made a permanent mark on my heart too. She was in a bad accident as an infant and became paralyzed from the chest or waist down. Week after week she would come early to class and make my day. She always had a big smile on her face and she knew I was excited to see her. If you ever wonder why people with the biggest hardships and struggles have the biggest smiles I think it's because they know they have an extra close relationship and need for the lord. The need for Him draws us so close to Him.

Anyway, it was the first time back after Christmas and she

couldn't wait to tell me what she got for Christmas. A new wheelchair that tilts up so she can actually see over the countertop. I was so happy for her but really needed her to share her excitement with the class. I told her my stories are mine and she needs to share hers too. It changed everyone in the room, listening to her made everyone less afraid to be her friend. Sometimes people shy away from those with these struggles especially at that age. Maybe it's because we feel like we don't know what to say and can feel the grace but don't know how to react. Not sure, maybe God is testing us and needing us to grow in compassion and kindness. I have so much admiration for people with lives like this, they show so much mercy for all of us around them. She died when she was about 19 or 20 and her funeral was beautiful. I could picture her flying and running and singing Gods praises with the light of heaven. I have no doubt that she went straight to heaven. I have seen her brother in church often and he is always sits in the very front. Thank you, Jesus, for these special brothers and sisters made everyone less afraid to be her friend. Sometimes people shy away from those with these struggles because they have an exceptional amount of grace that makes us feel like we don't know what to say. She died when she was about 19 or 20 and her funeral was beautiful. I could picture her flying and running and singing Gods praises with the light of heaven. I have no doubt that she went straight to heaven. I have seen her brother in church often and he is always in the very front. Thank you, Jesus, for these special brothers and sisters of mine.

> 2 Corinthians 16-18 *Therefore, we are not discouraged; rather, although our outer self is wasting away, our inner self is being renewed day by day. For this momentary light affliction is producing for us an eternal weight of glory beyond all comparison, as we look not to what is seen but to what is unseen; for what is seen is transitory, but what is unseen is eternal.*

# Wanna do a talk on the rosary?

So, one night at class I was asked to do a talk on the rosary. It was for the middle school kids and there were close to a hundred or more there. Are you picturing this? A bunch of seventh and eighth graders? After a long day at school, their favorite thing is to come to religion class. My Confirmation kids came with me to give me crap and distract me and of course give me their moral support. I probably should've done more research on the history but yea... My history was while my mom was sick, we would pray the rosary many times a day. People who aren't Catholic might think this is pointless. But actually, before Jesus died on the cross HE gave us one last command and that was to behold our mother. He knew her place in the grand plan and also knew her extreme love. He loved us so much to suffer and give up His life but her suffering was probably just as bad. She had to watch. She knew this was for our redemption. Her obedience was for all of us and we ask for her intercession because Jesus can't say no to His Mother. She wants only the best for her children. It was through Mary that our redeemer was brought to us. She was chosen to teach us and love us and bring us the Christ. The king of kings and Lord of Lords. She is so close to my heart and it was easy to talk about the rosary. It honors the life of her son. Something I just learned at mass this last weekend was the last words given by Mary in the Bible were "Do whatever He tells you" they were spoken at the wedding feast at Cana. She was used to encourage Jesus and get Him going with

His mission. It's the same for us. She tells us just like she told the servants, "Do whatever He tells you" … that is how we can come to understand our purpose. First, we have to have a relationship and knowledge of Our Lord, then we are able to do whatever He tells us. That's a good Mom! Someone who believes in you and shoves you out of the nest so you fulfill your plan and use your gifts. We all have a mission. The rosary is a prayer but even more it's a meditation. We fall into a deeper kind of prayer while praying with our mother. It's no coincidence that they call the long pass... Going deep... The Hail Mary. When we pray the Hail Mary and especially the rosary we are going deep. Throwing down some deep prayers. I finished talking to the kids and realized once again the Holy Spirit had my back! I didn't have to worry. God knows I don't take Him for granted!! I just rely on Him for everything that's all. Haha I sat down at the table with my class and we were going to make some rosaries and I looked down at mine and the chain of it turned to a dull gold color. My sister had this happen while praying for my mom (which I may have already told you) so I've seen it happen before. I always thought that this particular rosary would be easy to tell if it ever turned gold because it was made of clear beads and a silver chain. I was a little bit stunned and didn't know what to do. Inside me I heard I didn't do it for you silly girl. I did it for them. You need to show them. So, I started to show those around me and sure enough soon everyone saw the wonders of our night. Jesus loves His mother and needs us to love her too.

Hebrews 13:8 *Jesus Christ is the same yesterday, today and forever*

# *Shower thee people you love with love...*

This story is another kind of funny confirmation class story. It's a two- year combo story. I'll try and condense it (probably won't happen). Ok I was in class as usual and I was having a difficult time connecting with the kids on this particular evening and decided to stop and tell them a story.

It happened the year before and it was springtime and we were getting close to confirmation. The challenge with confirmation is that the devil, evil spirits etc. don't hold back from distracting the kids and basically harassing them all during their formation. They are at a very critical time in their lives anyway, 15 years old on average, and have a big decision to make! Whose team do you want to play for?? The devil will convince you that his team is more fun and might even make you popular but my answer to that is where do you want to spend eternity? This is a short time of existence and eternity is forever. Wanna play for a winner? Or join the losers in the world of sad lives. They all started out having fun but in no time, they end up making choices that can affect their life forever. I'm not saying they can't be forgiven for their mistakes, and get back on track to happiness, and holiness with the goal... joy. But they would have to acknowledge that they want to switch teams. God desires His children to play for him. He does give us the free will to choose and our free will is our big gift from God.

He believes in us, our choices matter, so why not pick the winning team from the get go.

Anyway, back to ninth grade. Big decisions... I brought a book with me to class that night that was called "Do whatever love requires" I was reading a paragraph and was going to discuss it. Of course, you know who wanted no part of it. Distractions everywhere. I kept going and got to a place where it said, "whoever has eyes and can see... Look now, whoever has ears and can hear listen! Listen now" and as if on cue the radiators, that should not have been on because it was warm outside, started to bang real loudly. I had to shout the rest of my sentence. It was super odd and it was one of my kids, Josh that hollared "it's a sign!! God wants us to listen!!" And it stopped message received! The best part was that I didn't deliver it. Josh had! God was giving a serious message of urgency. Don't wait! Choose to live for Him and you will never be sorry. Your adventure, your life will have purpose and meaning. So, the Angels on the radiators made an impact on all of us and delivered the message wonderfully.

Fast forward to the next year. We are in class and I'm trying to battle the distractions. I decided to tell the radiator story. They liked it with minimal enthusiasm. The next week came and it seemed like every day was Wednesday. "Ok Lord, what are we going to do tonight? These kids need you and I know they are battling. What should I do? Help me Jesus! This was my time of prayer and I always turned off my radio in the car on my way to class. Otherwise I had it on, I think I sound good when I sing with the radio, just don't turn it off. Haha anyway, I was praying away and my mind had been telling me all week that I should pray over each student one at a time and go out on a limb a bit. Step out of the box, leave my comfort zone. They were used to me praying all the time but I felt unworthy to pray over them. These thoughts were running through my head all week. I kept telling God that they would think I'm crazy. He would answer me with, since when do you care what people think? Hmm true. Anyway,

I'm in my car and almost to school. I was comfortable letting the Holy Spirit guide my evenings and things were better if I didn't over plan. So, this loud thought was suddenly very urgent. Turn on the radio! No this is my prayer time! Turn it on now! Ok, ok you don't have to yell. I turned on the radio and the song by James Taylor was on and it was just at the part "shower thee people you love with love show them the way that you feel. Things are going to work out better if you only will DO AS I SAY" So I'm pretty sure what I have to do.

When I got to class and everybody settled in we said our prayer and I just sat there looking at them. They were oddly quiet and asked what was going on. Now remember they just heard the radiator story the week before. I told them the Lord was asking me to do something with them but I didn't really feel like doing it, you're going to think I'm crazy for sure. Then you know what happened? You guessed it, the radiators went crazy. So funny is our Lord!! One kid hollared you have to do it! Of course, the noise stopped. They asked what God was asking and I told them. But I said I've never done that and I don't feel worthy. The same kid said, " why don't we just stand in a line like we are going to communion and you pray over us and we will all be quiet and pray for that person too?" I already had tears in my eyes, this was one of those many moments God was really blessing me. These children of His are so awesome. Remember these were the tough ones that were giving me trouble. Every soul is a precious child of God. All God was asking was to shower them with love. God is love, we just need to pray for each other.

Everyone was up for it so we did what was asked. It was a night I'll always remember. The Lord poured out of all of us. Tears were flowing. We all knew we were experiencing Jesus in a special way. It was all silent prayer but the love came through loud and clear.

When we were all done we sat in our usual circle pretty amazed. One girl asked what are we going to do now? Tell us a story! And one of the guys said "what do you mean? We are a story she will be telling students for years and years!" This was almost the best part. Because recognizing God alive and working for us in big and little ways was my mission. It's receiving that is all that's asked of us. Be open to receiving!! Confirmation comes with wonderful gifts of the Holy Spirit. Wisdom, understanding, good counsel, courage, knowledge, piety, awe and wonder and fear of the Lord. Which really means love for the lord. He wants us to have it all. Sometimes that's my prayer, "I'm not asking for much lord, I just want it all" haha He knows what I mean. I'm open to receiving everything. Don't let me miss a thing!! And it's a huge gift to me when these great brothers and sisters of mine teach me to never doubt His plan! It's always the best. It's not always the easiest but it's always the best. Thank you, Jesus, for everything. I can't get enough of your love. Hey, I think that's a song too!

> 2 Timothy 1:6-8 *For this reason, I remind you to stir into flame the gift of God that you have through the imposition of my hands. For God did not give us a spirit of cowardice but rather of power and love and self-control. S,o do not be ashamed of your testimony to our Lord, nor of me, a prisoner for his sake; but bear your share of hardship for the gospel with the strength that comes from God*

# Scott's angel

One of the really great things about sharing what God does for you, is that it frees other people to share what God does for them. My confirmation kids would figure out after just a few of my stories that these are things the Lord wants them to know and receive for themselves. He is working in their lives too!!

So here is Scott's story. We had finished a great class and lots of the time kids would stay late to keep the conversation going. I loved that, because as we all know we can't get too much Jesus. The topic that night was angels and their place in our lives. Our guardian angel and the relationship we can have with him or her... Recognizing how often we just miss getting hurt "just in time." How the word coincidence rips God off and all the hard work of His Angels. Remembering you are never alone that the Holy Spirit dwells within you and how comforting and empowering that is. Negative thoughts are never from God and angels need to be asked for their assistance. Except our guardian angel, they are always on duty as much as they can be and still allow us our free will. So many hundreds and hundreds of angels are around us in the unseen world and they won't barge in, at least not the holy angels. Because we all know the evil spirits are always trying to trip us up and ruin us, so we don't accomplish our mission and purpose for this earth life.

So, on this particular night, Scott stayed to tell me his story. About how much fun he and his friends had on their snowmobiles and ice fishing. I listened for a while then said "wait a minute! Are you telling me there are 18 ninth graders on snowmobiles? On the lake?" He said " yea!!" He laughed because he knew what I was thinking. I said, "well thanks for telling me, I now have something new to pray for." He laughed and told me to have a nice week. The next week came and Scott was there early and all hyper and excited to tell me something. What, what? So, first thing he wanted to know was whether or not I did actually pray for them. I said, "umm of course!" He was pleased to know that and this is when it gets interesting.

Scott was out with his two buddies after dark "doing the ditches" and was not able to keep up with them. They were way ahead of him because for some reason his machine was slow. He ended up burying his machine in a big drift and was stuck. It wouldn't budge. He sat alongside the two-lane highway and watched headlights come.... then taillights go... (This was years before cell phones.) He was nervous about who might stop and help him. All the fears and thoughts that run through your mind when you're all alone, its dark and cold. Then he remembered the angels need to be asked. His guardian angel needed help. So, he said "God if ever there was a time I need some angel's help I think it's now" he waited a little bit longer and all of a sudden, a corvette pulled over. Right there I had to stop him. Everyone knows people don't drive corvettes in the winter. He laughed and said "I know!! But just wait." So, he continued to tell me what happened. Out of the car came a man and woman both very beautiful and dressed for summer. The man was super buff and the woman had a sundress on. They didn't say very much. She got back in the car and pulled it around to face the ditch so they could see better. All the man said was, "its ok we'll get you out." Scott was doubtful it was so buried. The skis were sticking up out of the snow, it was real stuck. He told the man how badly it was stuck and he seemed a little annoyed. "I said we will get you out" he told him. And without very much effort he pulled the machine out of the drift. Scott was amazed. And the look on his face while telling this story was so funny. Shear amazement and joy. It was just what we had talked about. He said the best part of the story was his buddies pulled up just as the guy unstuck the snowmobile and was getting back in his car. They were all about the corvette. I guess the night before they were debating between the corvette and the Ferrari. Scott liked the corvette. They had no idea Scott was stuck and sure took long enough to realize he wasn't with them. Scott was so thankful and when he turned to tell them thanks again and goodbye they were gone. No taillights. End of story. So cool. Also, pretty cool that the friends came just in time, it validates the story. Sometimes, actually lots of times people need proof. I did tell Scott it would be nice to share this with the class. He did reluctantly, it's kind of risky to appear too religious in front of your peers. Not sure why that, maybe it's the devil trying to keep all the good stuff from getting out. Anyway, Angels exist and they love to help. They are among us, just because we don't get to see them, doesn't mean they aren't there. Happy is the day we get to see them.

Make sure to thank them, they are always around to do marvelous things for us and ask nothing in return. They are the most obedient servants of God with only our best interests in mind. When things don't seem to be going well and only bad things are happening…ask for help and protection from the Holy Angels. Sometimes it's a battle to get rid of the disobedient ones. (trying to be nice here) Everything we need is only a prayer away.

Thank you, Jesus, and help us be better aware of your Holy angels.

> Psalms 103:19-20 *The Lord has set his throne in heaven; his dominion extends over all. Bless the Lord, all you his angels, mighty in strength, acting at his behest, obedient to his command.*

# Grandma Gert

What a character was my Grandma Gert. She liked to call herself G.G. I think she knew she was a character, being my only Grandma, my dad's mother, I had no one to compare her to...I had my friend's grandmas, but let's just say Grams wasn't traditional. We would get to stay overnight with she and grandpa every so often, I especially loved staying at the lake. Waking up with the sound of mourning doves and the splash of the lake was the best. The special treat she always had for us was frozen waffles in her special toaster that made a ticking sound that eventually popped the waffles straight up in the air. Twas a riot.

I learned a lot from my grandma, she laughed and took life not too seriously. She chain-smoked and had a highball every afternoon...followed by a nap. The day my grandpa passed away was the first time I ever saw grandma cry. It was right before Christmas and Grandpa had just sold his liquor store that day. He was at our house and wanted to ride the snowmobile. My dad was going out to feed the chinchillas (another story, another day) and noticed Grandpa had just fallen over. For some reason, my mom was looking outside and heard dad holler to call the ambulance. A blizzard had suddenly come up and the ambulance took nearly four hours to get to our house. Grandpa had been dead immediately but my dad wouldn't let him go. He worked on him until the ambulance finally arrived. It was Dec. 21 the shortest day of the year, it seemed like the longest day ever. I was eight, and grandpa was 58.

After finishing beauty school, I moved back to my hometown and that's when Grandma and I grew close. Every week I would pick her up to do her hair, of course she smoked while I did her hair and for some reason it didn't bother me. She was a stubborn lady and if she saw a no smoking sign she would light up…nobody could tell her she couldn't smoke. Of course, lots of life happened during those years doing Grandma's hair. She taught my girls how to play cards and appreciate the little things. She had a way of never worrying. I would talk to her about my faith and she would just say that she didn't want to talk about that. She was a believer and a church goer and taught me that just because you don't talk about it doesn't mean you aren't a believer. She trusted

I never heard my Grams complain. Every now and then she would tell me that she was annoyed about something. Like the time she had a lump in her breast? Yea, I asked her how long she had it and I guess it had been there about a year…so quickly we made the appointment and she had a mastectomy. It was cancer. No biggie, the lady came to council her on "her loss" shortly after her surgery and the only trouble Grams said she was having was she didn't know where to keep her kleenex anymore. She could be quite the crack up that's for sure. How about the day during a game of bridge with her girlfriends, her "falsie" fell out of her bra, which was a shoulder pad she had taken out of a blouse, this was the eighties after all. It plopped onto the table which provided everyone a good laugh. She never complained. Not even when her chemo pills were messing with her and she decided she couldn't have her highballs anymore. Imagine quitting just like that cold turkey, never to mention it again. The big one though was her smoking. She was over eighty years old and had gall bladder surgery. It was pretty hard on her and she had to stay in the hospital for a couple of weeks. She couldn't believe they wouldn't let her smoke. She went those two long weeks without her cigs and never picked them up again. No complaining, well just once when I brought it up. I mentioned that her eyes seemed so much clearer since she quit smoking. She told me that she knew it and it didn't make her one bit happy. I could go on and on about Grams. She was something else. When the doctors told her that her aneurism had grown a tiny bit. Half a centimeter or something. She told them she wanted a second opinion when they suggested surgery. She was at least 85 by this point. Pretty hard of hearing and her sight was minimal too. She was still living at home alone and never drove so we didn't have to take the car away at least. I mentioned that to her that it was lucky she didn't drive, that was one less adjustment that she had to deal with. She said, "very funny." The doctor told her that she could get another opinion but that thing in her stomach could go at any time. She looked at him and said, "Wouldn't that be a good way to go?" Grams was never lacking for words; her quick wit was always sharp.

Then one day I got a call, it was Grams. I was in the middle of cleaning closets, up to my knees is clothes when I heard Grams in a very urgent voice, "quick get over here!" I had always dreaded the day when I would walk into her house and find her lying in a heap or something. I'm not your girl when it comes to emergencies, I panic to put it mildly. I didn't even ask why, I just said I would be right there. It took about 3 minutes to get to her place and there she was with a look on her face that I'll remember forever. She said, "He was here! Grandpa was here!! Standing exactly where you are right now!" "Cool Grams" was all I could say. She asked me what I thought he wanted, he didn't say anything. I said, "Well, he probably is letting you know to get ready...your time is probably coming." She said, "that's probably why I'm going through his closet." He had died 38 years prior and she never went through his stuff. Maybe that's why she never worried, she avoided unpleasantness, some might call that living in denial, but maybe denial isn't all bad. She definitely didn't borrow trouble. Anyway, she wanted me to take all of Grandpa's stuff and keep it. I said I would. When I left, she asked me in a very sincere and soft tone, "Do you think I was dreaming?" I said, "Well, I don't know…were you sleeping?" She looked at me and said, "No." I said, "Well then I don't think it was a dream, it was just Grandpa letting you know he will be here for you and the Lord is allowing you some time to prepare. It could be years or it could be days. Either way you are doing what is being asked. You are getting ready." She seemed calm and gave me a big hug. I told my dad about this and he was able to go stay with her. I mentioned to grams that she might want to think about a nursing home, but quickly got shot down. She told me she would let me know when she was ready for that. It does pay to be a little stubborn.

I was so glad dad stayed with Grams because in a few short days he called me to tell me she fell into his arms coming down her stairs. Those stairs were always in my nightmares. He called the ambulance and I got there before they did. She was unconscious but as they were taking her out of the house on the gurney she opened her eyes to tell the EMT that he was so handsome. (a few too many harlequin romance novels) I didn't have the heart to tell him she had little to no vision. The picture I have of them wheeling her out of the house still keeping her humor is a precious memory. The best part of this story is still coming.

We had a very tough afternoon. She didn't, but my cousins and my sisters and my dad and uncles had to say our goodbyes. It truly was a good way to go and she was blessed. She passed away later that night after living 88 years. I do remember saying to her while she laid there sleeping, too bad you smoked Grams you would still have ten more years. I think I was trying to be funny one last time. Imagine, with all that she had going against her she kept her faith by not worrying and keeping her humor. Maybe that is the cure for all that ails us…faith and humor.

She had the last word though, when I got to the adoration chapel that Wednesday evening, and knelt at the kneeler where I always do, there to my surprise was a prayer card of St. Gertrude.

She had never been to the chapel and had no idea I went there every Wednesday night. Only God would know how to give me this gift from Grams. It was like she was letting me know she was there and thanked me for all the stories and all our special times together. Being a hairdresser comes with many special gifts. It can be quite the vocation.

I was so thankful for that wonderful gift from God. He knew how much I wanted my Grams to receive Him fully into her heart…It was her sign that she made it!

Thank you, Jesus, for loving us.

> Romans 13:7-9 *None of us lives for oneself. For if we live, we live for the Lord, and if we die, we die for the Lord; so then, whether we live or die, we are the Lord's. For this is why Christ died and came to life, that he might be Lord of both the dead and the living.*

# They are deer to me

This story is one that I will also never forget. You know when you get too intense? No matter what the situation is, you blow it out of proportion and make too big a deal out of it? Ya, that happens to me sometimes and it usually goes on for a while before I realize I'm doing it.

We lived in the country, and it took about ten minutes to get to town. The house we lived in, we built and it was very nice. On a very normal day, I was driving the girls to school. Anna was in 5th or 6th grade and Laura was in kindergarten. I was intensely trying to make a point to Anna about something. I think I used up all ten minutes of the drive on my teaching moment. When I got to Anna's school, she got out of the car and I, in my cheerful voice, said have a great day... Um yea she just listened to me rant for the last ten minutes, and now I'm telling her to have a nice day. She had to start her day with so much information. Stuff that could've been said in maybe two minutes but I needed all ten. If George had been there he would've said, "Quit kickin' the dead dog." It was lent and I had asked God to help me give up hollering. I thought that was maybe something more productive than my usual chocolate. Anna looked at me with a look like, yea ok, and she told me to have a good day too. I could cry. But that's not the worst of it. Laura looked at me and with her kindergarten voice and said, " mom, you shunt of guv up hollering for lent you're not doing so good" I looked at her with a sad look and said "do you think I was too hard on Anna?" She nodded her head yes and I dropped her off at her school. She told me she loved me and I was almost in tears. I am not worthy Lord.

Ok so on my way home I started screaming at my Lord. I was yelling (sounds crazy) at Him and asking Him to help me. I want to quit yelling and feeling so intense. Of course, God is His awesome love was wanting this for me too. Because, just then a couple of beautiful deer walked right out in front of my car. I was in the middle of a residential area, and had never seen deer there or near there before. The two of them stopped right in front of me, I had come to a complete stop and we had a stare down. They were literally touching my bumper. We had eye contact long enough for me to hear my loud thought which was "don't forget to appreciate their beauty for they are dear to me." Oh ok!! The message came through loud and clear. They are His and be thankful for all of the beautiful things they bring to my life. My teaching moments don't have to be so intense. Just love them.

I sat in my car after pulling over and cried in such awe. My love for the Lord is overwhelming me. I am once again humbled by all that He is and does for me. He wanted me to quit yelling too. I wrote both the girls a letter that day. Praising and thanking God for them. I apologized for how crazy I had been for those few months and so thankful for Gods message to me. They are "deer" to our Lord even more "deer" than they are to me. That seems impossible but with God all things are possible.

Another funny story about our house in the country. I was in confirmation class with my ninth graders, it was the year Anna was in my class. Time was flying by. We were talking about the man that came up to Jesus and asked Him "Lord what do I need to do to get to heaven?" Our Lord answered him. "The Ten Commandments" He said "I already do that" Jesus said " well then sell what you have and come follow me" Hmmm, that one is a toughie ... He had a lot of worldly things and of course Jesus knew that. He left Jesus sad. He couldn't do it. He was the only one in the bible that walked away from our lord sad. We discussed this and I heard myself telling them that it's not that God doesn't want us to have stuff. He wouldn't have created nice things if He didn't want us to enjoy them. It's just that we can't make things bigger and more important that He is in our lives, He put Himself as the number one command for a reason. I heard myself say "things like volleyball or hockey" and in my mind, I heard "your house" ... Oh yea that's what I thought too. It wasn't that God didn't want us to have the house we built, but it was bigger than we needed and took up too much of our time and we stressed about it. When I got home I said to George "guess what I think we are supposed to do?" He said, " sell the house" I was shocked. He knew it too. That's what I love about George, he is a listener and a believer and doesn't think I'm crazy. Though he doesn't talk about it out loud very often…imagine if we both talked this much…Anyway, we put the house on the market and the third people through it bought it. We tried to talk them out of it. Secretly neither of us wanted to move. But there they were. We became very good friends and that shouldn't shock us either. God brings people together and rarely cares about things. He's all about the people true? We ended up buying and moving into the house of some good friends. It was the house where George and I met. Remember right in the driveway? That house had been for sale for over a year and nobody could believe it wasn't selling. I concluded that it was because we were supposed to have it. Pray, pray, pray, trust and believe…

> Sirach 1:26-27 *If you desire wisdom, keep the commandments, and the Lord will bestow her upon you; For the fear of the Lord is wisdom and discipline; faithfulness and humility are his delight.*

# Happy graduation Laura

Getting ready for a grad party is all consuming. It's full of emotions. Huge milestones and too much change for this mother. One of the perks with our greenhouse business is we have an abundance of flowers. We had Anna's party in the backyard and of course it was beautiful. Now it's Laura's turn, are you serious? How can this be happening?

I miss my Mom every day, but it's these special times I really miss her. Like I could use some of her wisdom and encouragement. I guess most days are like that.

It's good therapy to work in the dirt, so getting the yard ready helped a lot. We have a small pagoda in our yard and for Anna's party we had wild roses growing and on the morning of her party I noticed two little roses bloomed which were a comfort to me. I knew my mom was near and helping us get through it all. So, for Laura's reception, I was hoping for a sign for her too. Pretty typical of a second born, middle girl of three girls, I never want anybody to feel left out. I wouldn't want her to feel slighted. Jeepers how God must roll his eyes at me!

So many things were running through my mind. Memories like I remember hiking in our state park with George and the girls. Laura was two and needed me to carry her. We were enjoying the fresh air and I decided to ask her a few questions. I asked if she remembered Nama or knew her from heaven before she got here. She nodded that she did. I asked her what she was like and she said hugs.

That made sense to me, Nama would've been so full of hugs for her Laura. I asked if she knew grandpa Roy... Remember she was born on his birthday. She made this crazy noise with her mouth. This was truly something because he died when I was eight and the thing I remember most was this crazy noise he would make with his mouth. It sounded exactly like the noise Laura just made. Very cool. Then there were the regular memories, it's like your life flashes right before your eyes when your babies graduate. Laura learning how to ride her bike, or the day she decided she was okay and didn't need me to walk her up to the school building. Or here's a good one. The day she got her license, she was so nervous. Here comes another mini story...

We had a pretty tough examiner everyone called Sarge, and she just knew she would get her. She wasn't afraid to flunk people. Laura also worried that too many people knew she was taking her test and what if she didn't pass. I reassured her that not many people knew, and when we went to get in the car to leave, the painters on the ladder painting the house hollered, "Good luck Laura!" Oh my gosh, even the painters knew. I thought this was a little bit funny, but when she asked me to pray over her I knew she was serious. I said a prayer that the lord would give her a peaceful feeling, because she was a good driver. She was still nervous because she couldn't feel any peace. It told her it wasn't going to happen until she needed it. We sat in the room with the others all taking it for the second time, one kid was taking it for the third time. Finally, it was her turn and long story short, I know too late, she passed! The best part was (for me) was that she was so excited to tell me she felt peace the minute she strapped on her seatbelt. Yay, so awesome. Another crazy thing is that my friend Mary Beth gave me a tee shirt that day that said, "Jesus, He gives us what we need when we need it." This is so true; how often do we pray for things to happen and say our prayers weren't answered...when the answer comes when it's the perfect time. Amazing Grace

Anyway, with Laura graduating I'm freaking out as bad if not worse than when Anna graduated. Empty nest issues. So, it's the night before the party and we had the craziest spring. We had snow in May and it was lots of snow. All of our plants were really late. The peonies that usually blossom at least by the first week in June had not even started. The buds were there but had not cracked any color at all. Peonies have lots of ants on them and I learned that the ants are what open the flower. Who knows, the ants were probably still underground afraid to come out. Afraid it might snow again. So, the night before the party, we were finishing up what we had to in the yard. I was sad about the peonies because they are my favorite. We have about six big plants around our yard and they all were closed tighter than a drum. Of course, all things are possible in my Lord Jesus so I asked Him to please open my favorite peach peony as a gift to Laura. A sign that Nama and our loved ones on the other side would be there. Just a little crack of color Lord. I forgot about my prayer but was I so excited when I woke up the next day. I was setting up our beautiful garden party. Praying in thanksgiving for the many blessings my mind still flooded with memories and wishing my Mom could be here. How much she missed and we missed too. Then something just called my eyes over to the peach peony. It was in full bloom! Not just a little crack of color but every blossom was a beautiful rich peach color. None of my other peonies had even a crack of color started. I had a good cry and we had the best day and of course I had to share this story with everyone who came. I learned so long ago that these miracles are for everyone and they must be shared. Thank you, Jesus! Thank you for loving us all the same. And I love you Mom, thanks for coming and reminding us you are always so near. That veil is so thin.

> Ephesians 3:20-21 *Now to him who is able to accomplish far more than all we ask or imagine, by the power at work within us, to him be glory in the church and in Christ Jesus to all generations, forever and ever. Amen*

# It's all about the egg

So, I couldn't get through this project and not mention my absolute, no question about it, can't ever let it go feelings about abortion.

It's a subject most people avoid, but I can't. I have many people that I know that have been involved with abortion, either very personally because they have had one, or they have been a nurse in a clinic and witnessed them or they had a girlfriend who had one. In every case, it changed their lives and in many cases, they never got over it. It is for them that I feel for the most.

The lie is that it is the easy way out, the simple solution and that you get your life back. If only that were true. I feel, and this is my opinion, that the reason families and relationships and the world is hurting is because we are buying into the lie. Because of this we don't have to change our behavior and wounds are happening everywhere. Women or should I say society is hurting because we are going against nature. It is unnatural for a woman to kill her child. We try to convince ourselves that it isn't a child, but deep down we all know the truth. We try to block it out but we know.

My good friend worked in a women's clinic back when abortions were first happening. She got to work one day and much to her surprise the doc was performing an abortion right in front of her eyes. She quit her job that day, she has not been able to get the picture of the baby's parts all over the table that had to be inventoried…to make sure they got it all. It was a late term baby. From the beginning, babies of all ages have been murdered inside their mothers and these women have to remember the sounds and smells forever. It is unnatural.

The argument is always that it is a woman's right to choose, but it is the innocent little child that has to feel the pain, they have no choice. I believe, that it is no wonder that we have a killing problem, not a gun problem, but a lack of love for life. It is no wonder that our world suffers, we have chosen to kill the most innocent. The ripple effect of abortion is an overall lack of love and respect for all life.

For me, because I was not able to get pregnant, I have kept this issue close to my heart. One time, while cutting hair for a young adult girl, she was explaining how she was planning to go with her sister for her abortion. I had so much urgency within myself to save this little person. I had statistics and information that I didn't know I even knew. I felt like it was a spiritual battle unlike any other. Please choose life!! There are millions of couples on lists all over the country waiting and crying every night just like me. Maybe you're asking the question, "why didn't we adopt her baby?" because it wasn't legal at that time, had we been related maybe possibly, but the world tells us the easy solutions is to get rid of it.

So, It's all about the egg...

Let's talk about something that is natural. Lots of times while in confirmation class with my kiddos, things would just come out of my mouth that I had never thought of before. I thought of those moments as holy spirit lessons for me. That's where some of my theories would come from.

When thinking about a young girl going through puberty growing into a woman and all the years until menopause, her body is all about the egg. This is a topic I've never been afraid to talk about because my body was a mystery and had me trying to figure it out for many years. Though I probably focused on it too much but it also taught me a lot of understanding about the physical and emotional wellbeing of being female. While reading this try to picture my poor ninth graders having to listen, it's funny.

It's not hard to understand, we just never take the time to really think about it. The nature of being a girl. Sometimes it starts way before the first period ever comes. You might be in fifth or sixth grade and you begin to pudge up around the middle just a little. Mother may tell you to lay off the sweets but that seems to be the only thing you want to eat. Poor mom doesn't even think about why, until that one day when you have a huge emotional outburst over…. nothing? wait, what just happened…Oh…mom is being made somewhat aware but may still be in denial. Until a couple of weeks or months later and it happens again, this can go on for a year or two actually. The body is preparing for the egg.

Then the magical month happens, the hips are in place, the body has made many changes and to a girl, they all seem like negative changes. We become so self -conscience and emotional. It's ok, it's ok, it is such a wonderful gift that you are being given and so very sad that we call it the monthly curse or worse. We should call it the cross instead, at least that would remind us that we never carry the cross alone. It is something we shouldn't take for granted. The body is so delicately made, just picture in our minds what really is going on.

All month long, every month the body is preparing for the egg. It was created in a beautiful way to protect and nurture the egg. Keep in mind this only happened to me a few times so I am going with what the holy spirit was teaching, and my girlfriends once told me. For part of the month, we seem fine, then a twinge is felt on one side or the other. This can be easily ignored. A few days go by and we might have lots of energy and emotions are feeling good. This is ovulation. Who thinks about all of this? Probably no one. So, let's think… together. Ok, the egg is on the move, the body automatically puffs up to protect the egg and is excited about what could happen. Creation is all God. Now this is when I tell the kids, He did give us a brain, and wants nothing but love and good things for us. It's the evil one who gets into our heads and talks us into stupid stuff. Family is God's most treasured gift and it's the most attacked. When you think of the problems in our world, it's when we reject the love of God. Prayer people…remember it's our weapon. Anyway, the egg is on the move and the body is all about taking care of it. Lots going on, the female body was created for this. Most months the body is disappointed and the egg has to leave. The Body has to sluff off all the protection, it contracts and is sad. Women get hassled because they are having PMS and experiencing anger, sickness and lots of other feelings that vary. She eventually feels ok and for a few days can go about business as usual, but in no time, the egg is on the move again.

Now, imagine the egg after it was fertilized! The body knows just what to do!! It's busy building cells by the thousands and we don't even know we are pregnant yet…Happily building. The tiny creation is on a mission from the very beginning…fighting for its life. Its natural instinct is to live and grow. It's the woman's instinct to protect and nurture it. It's our nature. Embrace and love this gift. It is also true for many that this comes at a very inconvenient time and some may even say unwanted… God wants all His creation. What nobody will say is that this child of God was created for someone and we need to think about why this happened. If you didn't plan this for life than it happened for someone else. This child is a gift if not for you for someone and it is a gift from God every time.

To summarize, back to my original point. No child is a mistake, we are all God's creation from the very first cell of our being, until we pass away at the age of 99 years. There is a plan and purpose for each and every life. It's not ours to decide what that is, only God knows the plan. The hardest part is trusting the plan. If you are having trouble trusting, this is the time for prayer. After all, we are all, always, a child of God. That is our identity.

*Romans 12:12 Rejoice in hope, endure in affliction, persevere in prayer*

# And what about my broken zipper theory

Mom used to say that prayer is like bringing your broken zipper to God. Think of yourself as a small child. I remember this happening to me when I was about three or four. I got all dressed to go outside to play in the snow. Big bulky snowsuit. Snow pants, hat, scarf, mittens and boots. The only way to enjoy the winter is to dress for it!! Anyway, so you know what happens next, the minute you get outside, you have to go potty. You ignore it, but you're three, and it doesn't go away. You go to the door and bang on it because the mittens make it tough to turn the knob. Then Mom comes to the door and asks what I need. At this point, I'm doing the dance and can't explain fast enough. Laughingly, she would let me in. Mittens would come off and sure enough my zipper is stuck. I mean super stuck!! First words are HELP ME!! She was always right there and her first words would be "well, let go, let me see if I can help!!" I'm trying frantically to work the zipper AND asking for help so once again she says, "let go!" I FINALLY surrender control. It had to get bad enough before I handed it over to her so she could get at it and fix it. Pretty sure I'm wetting my pants by this point.

Same thing with our prayers. We hollar, "HELP" but God can't even get close to our problem until we let go. This seems weird to us because if we let go of the worry then maybe God will think we don't care and will forget about it. Not true. He knows our needs before we do. He will be able to help and guide us if only we let Him. So, I picture God saying, "just stand still so I can help." There will be those desperate times when we have to cut a hole in the roof and lower our friend down, but when we stand still and let Him help, He can get at our broken zipper. Then… we can take care of business.

Yea that's what my mom used to say ♥ We called it the broken zipper theory. Let go and let God

Dependence on God… *Matthew 6:25-27*

*Therefore, I tell you, do not worry about your life, what you will eat or drink, or about your body, what you will wear. Is not life more than food and the body more than clothing? Look at the birds in the sky; they do not sow or reap, they gather nothing into their barns, yet your heavenly Father feeds them. Are not you more important than they? Can any of you by worrying add a single moment to your life-span?*

# Sam ...Are you coming with me?

My Story about Sam is still too hard to talk about, I wasn't sure I could even tell this part, but I think he would want me to.

You see, Sam is a very special person in our lives. One of the blessings of the Coffee Shop was meeting all sorts of people, I could write a whole book just about the shop. It was always a funny joke, the sitcom we could write... every day we came up with a new plot.

This is where I met Sam's family, and after selling the shop they asked if I would billet their oldest daughter Lyndsay, and their son Sam. After talking to George, we thought it was perfect because Laura would be going off to school and empty nester didn't sound appealing for us yet. We took these kids into our home and in about an hour they were in our hearts. Sam was with us for a couple of years and very quickly became a son/brother to us all. He and Lyndsay were very close and after she graduated, it was just us. Life is full of transitions and we are helped by the Lord when we open our hearts to others.

Sam was a very talented and good looking young man with a very pure spirit. There were times I would walk past his room and he would be on his knees in prayer. He would post lots of Instagram posts of his many escapades and had hundreds of "likes." The hockey life was important to him, he was talented and gifted with the most wicked slap shot out there. There wasn't anything he couldn't do. My favorite post of Sam's was the one where he was bowed in prayer in his full hockey gear with his favorite bible quote along the edge. Philippines 4:13 and Proverbs 16:3. He was the kind of kid liked to sit on the counter and talk about life. His appetite for food was almost as big as his appetite for life. I could go on and on but I better hold off in case his mom wants to write his story.

One thing Sam did was live life with lots of enthusiasm, like he was in a hurry… it's possible that his spirit knew his time on earth would be cut short.

So, after his death, and a funeral of about a thousand people, we all were left with a huge hole in our hearts. What are we going to do without our Sammy? His big smile and big love for each of us, he inspired us to be and do more. What are we going to do without Sam? What would we do without our faith? We ask this of ourselves every day. Lord carry me…

I'm very sure, people were put in our lives for a reason, and the mission for each of us is to love and this mission continues with a lot more intensity, after we leave this earth.

Out of nowhere, I get a job with the church…something I never thought about doing. I'm going into the hospital and nursing homes to visit the elderly and pray with them. Bringing them communion and also planning funerals with the families that are in extreme grief. I spent so many years with the youth and praying with them, this was very unexpected. I'm not very nursy and a little awkward in nursing homes, but you go where the Lord leads you right?

On my first day going into the hospital, I got out of my car and said out loud, "Well Sam, are you coming with me?" After visiting my last person, this little old lady said to me, "Are the two of you going to Mass now?" I was stunned! I said, "pardon me?" She repeated, "are the two of you going to mass now?" I was so thrilled with this gift from God. I replied, "yes we are" and left the hospital floating.

The last time Sam stayed at our house just a month before he passed, he came to church with us. Ever since, I can feel him with me when I'm at Mass. It's a gift and I am so thankful.

I miss you Sam, we all do… we love you too!

> *Philippines 4:13 I have the strength for everything though him who empowers me*
>
> *Proverbs 16:3 Entrust your works to the Lord, and your plans will succeed*
>
> *And I'm adding the next line…*
>
> *Proverbs 16:4 The Lord has made everything for a purpose*

# The nun run

My friend Ang and I were given the opportunity to chaperone a group of about ten girls, in a van, on a five-day trip called the nun run. It was an idea that our associate priest, Fr. Drew had, and if you spend any amount of time with him, you might just become a nun or a priest. He is a very inspired and gifted priest, who easily becomes your friend. He loves being a Priest, and is now a Bishop...God knew what He was doing in calling Fr. Drew, and though the trip was about learning the lives of these sisters in a variety of communities, we all learned so much on the road with our favorite priest. So many laughs and lots of joy.

This trip was back in 2002, when the church was going through some very hard times, and we drove through many states and hopefully regained hope and faith in the many people we came across. Our stops included Atchison KS, at the Immaculate Heart of Mary, then on to the Hospital Sisters of St. Francis, in Springfield IL, then to The Passionists Nuns of Kentucky, where they spend their days praying in silence for all of us and specifically priests and finally the Missionaries of Charity in Chicago. These communities were so beautiful and full of joy and peace and love. They owned a watch...they were all in full habits and the happiest people I have ever met. All of these communities were growing in numbers, lots of young women were visiting and I for one finally "got it". I think every catholic girl thinks about becoming a nun... at least for a day or two, but you think, no I could never do that, I want a family. After visiting these beautiful places, it once again taught me that you think you are sacrificing something but you cannot out give God! They were the happiest people and it gave me a little feeling of what heaven is like.

I'm writing about this trip because a couple of things happened to me, well actually many things reshaped me, but two things stick out in my mind and I think I'm supposed to share them. First, at the Passionists, we were to be in silence. They speak only 2 hours a day and I thought that was going to be hard for me…everyone thought that actually. Haha, it wasn't… and it was the moment we sat in the dining area that was floor to ceiling windows, overlooking the beautiful Kentucky hills, the Lord spoke to me. We were eating dinner and all the chairs were facing the windows, and it was obvious that it was time to hear from our Jesus. Tears began flowing down my cheeks, and it was as if I was all alone with my Lord. The things you can hear when you are finally in silence…amazing. It's no wonder the devil keeps us so busy and constantly plugged in.

We did get some time with one of the sisters, who knew Fr. Drew from NET MINISTRIES and the Mother of the community. One thing the mother said that stuck with me was, when we choose against our true vocation…whatever that is…this can cause disease. We have to stay close to God in prayer to understand our purpose and plan and to really understand our identity. We are a child of God. This is our identity. We had a little time to journal the next morning, after Mass and morning prayer. We were asked the question "why would anyone become a nun?" My daughter, Anna, who was the youngest one on our trip, said, "Well maybe they wouldn't feel complete otherwise" Little did we know we would be going to her best friend, Jillian's first vows with the Sisters of Life out in New York a few years later. This is a community we didn't get to visit, but it shows that God calls us where He wants us to be…when we listen and joy follows. Jills is now Sr. Magnificat Rose. What a celebration that was, so much joy on the faces of all those beautiful young women. I can't imagine the final vows. It will be amazing Grace for sure.

Anyway, back to my nun run, after leaving the beautiful Kentucky hills, we drove to the busy and crazy city of Chicago. We had so much peace and quiet and the chapel was so beautiful with over a hundred acres of trails that all lead to the cross. They pray for the world to always remember the Passion of Christ. I thought I would have trouble relating to this community but it was the most difficult one to leave. Going to the Missionaries of Charity was life changing as well. Their way is also an amazing sacrifice. They live like the poor. In America, they have to abide by our codes so electricity, plumbing etc. is required, but in many places around the world they go without many of these things. The little nun that I worked with had worked with Mother Theresa for years. She even looked like her. She had a great personality, with a humility like I'd never known. The soup kitchen was in full swing, we helped serve a couple hundred people and they rely solely on donations. They always have enough. It was a very hot and humid day in June, and I was sweating like crazy. The young mother of the house took one look at me and plugged in the fan. Here they were, in full habit and not feeling the heat and here I was about to pass out. What a wimp, I thought I was such a toughy. The fan felt great, and I was very thankful. The charism or purpose of their mission is to be Christ to others. That when you leave them, you have seen the face of Christ. They pray continually. A funny thing happened as we were cleaning up, they wash and scrub the pots like brand new, then bleach the towels and hang them to dry. This little nun (I wish I remembered her name) and I were just finishing the chores when Fr. Drew grabbed a clean towel to wipe out the garbage can and threw it back in the sink. She just looked at me with sparkling eyes and said, "Men". It was so cute we laughed and he had no idea why. After the work was done, many of the nuns go out to the streets to minister to the people. They are in one of the poorest neighborhoods and go out two by two. We were able to sit and visit a while with my little nun friend and the Mother, who did I mention was in her 30's? There is hope people!! We talked for a while and my little nun friend took a while to share some of her stories. She was the most humble person I have ever met. It was then that I found out she had worked with Mother Teresa. When it was time for us to leave, I was full of gratitude for having been in this place and especially meeting my little sister friend. She would like that I don't remember her name, it's all about Jesus. When I was shaking her hand, she held it in hers and looked me in the eyes and said nothing. Our eyes locked and tears immediately were flowing from my eyes. She knew exactly what happened. She didn't say a word, but smiled knowing I received a gift from our Lord. I saw Jesus in her eyes. It was the hardest thing to leave… His gaze…

One of the things that I learned was that when you pray with someone you bond with them in a way like no other. It is love, God is love, pray, pray, pray to stay in Love and serve in Love and grow in Love. Pray unceasingly

*Isaiah 12:2-4*

*God indeed is my salvation; I am confident and unafraid. For the Lord is my strength and my might, and he has been my salvation. With joy you will draw water from the fountains of salvation. And you will say on that day; give thanks to the Lord, acclaim his name; among the nations make known his deeds, proclaim how exalted is his name.*

# *Awe and Wonder*

I was wondering how I was going to wrap up this mission/project…
then it came to me! It's about the Fear of the Lord. The Holy Spirit
freely gives us gifts and it's there for all of us to accept. Our free
will once again comes into play. I'm sure you realize that I am a
Catholic, and I love my "religion" even during these times when
that word is unpopular. This is reminding me of another story but
I better just stop already…remind me when you see me if you want
to hear that one. Haha

Anyway, the word, religion has taken a hit these days, but
it is being misunderstood. Spirituality, which is most of what I
am writing about, is important to be able to see God and have a
relationship with Our love and Savior, Jesus. Religion, is a way
to be refueled and grow in community. To be able to go out and
share the love, be emptied by loving our neighbors and living in
service…only to go to back church, and repeat…

For me, receiving the sacraments is food for my spirit. I am
starving without Him. Our mission is not possible for us to do
alone. We were created in His image and likeness…God is love…
We were made to love. The Holy Spirit is the wind beneath our
wings, blessing us with gifts to form a relationship with us. Pay
attention, because unless we pay attention we miss out. These
gifts of courage, wisdom, right judgement (counsel) piety,
understanding, knowledge, and fear of the Lord which is also
known as Awe and Wonder. Why would we go through this life

rejecting these special gifts? I've heard from lots of people that we shouldn't need a sign, but to that I always say, "I know, but the Bible/ Jesus, uses signs all throughout. Jesus came here to show us how to live and He knows that in our weakness and humanness, we need signs. Pretty sure, this is one of my special gifts. Also pretty sure it is there for everyone. I know that because I am willing to spill by guts by sharing these signs, I feel like I am given more to share. Just like all the gifts of the Holy Spirit, the more we accept the more we are given. We cannot out-give God. If we are unsure and just beginning the journey, He knows that too. We cannot hide our hearts from our Lord. If you are the person that happened to pick up this book and read it, know that you are being prayed for. God uses people to speak to us. He has something to say to all of us. We have to move ourselves, just like the leper, he had to go dunk seven times, the paralytic had to get up!! Our job is to say a prayer, ask for help and Open the Eyes of our Hearts. Miracles happen...